Startup CTO

A Field Guide to Scaling up Your Company's Technology/Product Function

Matt Blumberg and Shawn Nussbaum

Bolster Network

Contents

III. CTO/CPO AND THE LEADERSHIP TEAM

Foreword

Scott Dorsey

As a first-time tech founder and CEO at ExactTarget, one phrase kept ringing through my head: "I don't know what I don't know." Even with 10+ years of business experience and a freshly minted MBA degree, I had so many blind spots having never built software, raised venture capital or even led a multi-functional organization. Filling in these gaps took many years and lots of trial and error.

One of my gap-filling strategies was to learn from other CEOs going through similar highs and lows of scaling their company. On this journey, I was fortunate to meet Matt Blumberg. As CEO of Return Path, Matt was building a high growth company in the same digital marketing industry as me. I was impressed by his leadership, strategic thinking, and commitment to helping other entrepreneurs. We became fast friends and we both looked forward to learning from one another.

Matt was always gracious and willing to take my call or have dinner together. Our conversations covered every topic imaginable from leadership to board management to strategic partnerships to international expansion. My advice to entrepreneurs and leaders––build your peer network and spend time developing and nurturing these relationships. While board members and advisors are an important source of knowledge, learning from peers can be invaluable.

One of the highlights of my relationship with Matt was when we were both invited to the White House to witness President Obama signing the Jumpstart our Business Startups Act (or JOBS Act) in April of 2012. With bi-partisan support, the law opened up crowdfunding for startups and streamlined the IPO path. ExactTarget had just gone public two weeks prior so I knew the benefits that the JOBS Act would bring to entrepreneurs. But what I didn't know in April 2012 was that the event would foreshadow my relationship with Matt and how we would work together supporting entrepreneurs and startup ecosystems.

Fast forward to 2020. We are facing unprecedented challenges in the world and the need for innovation and leadership has never been greater. CEOs and functional leaders need tools and resources to accelerate their learning curves and the learning curves of those around them. Speed of learning, thought, and action are more important now than ever. This is why I am so excited about Matt's latest book, *Startup CXO*.

Startup CXO provides a comprehensive field guide to starting and scaling tech companies. Really, the information is super helpful to any company. It provides a "book within a book" framework to enable and empower readers to jump into any section as needed. And it's written by practitioners who provide tons of tangible advice and actionable insights. By reading this book, I believe that leaders will be better equipped to build great companies and anticipate what's around every corner.

In my view, the best CEOs have a grasp of all functions. They can go a mile wide and a couple inches deep. They hire A+ talent and build a culture that brings out the very best in people. They understand how Sales and Marketing fit together, they value HR, Finance, and Legal and understand their interdependencies, they have a clear vision for how Product and Engineering fit together, they know how to be aggressive and how to manage risk, and so much more.

So, *Startup CXO* is an amazing resource for CEOs but also for functional leaders and professionals at any stage of their career. The best functional leaders and professionals understand that cross-functional teamwork is everything. It's so important to have insight and empathy for how other areas of the organization operate. The big picture is needed to see how all of the puzzle pieces fit together.

I feel so lucky that through our venture studio, High Alpha, I have the opportunity to work with Matt and his leadership team as we build

Bolster––a talent marketplace for startup and scaleup tech companies. We are living and applying the concepts and lessons contained in this very book!

My wish for you is that reading *Startup CXO* minimizes your "I don't know what I don't know" list; that it accelerates your development, your curiosity, your ability to ask the right questions, and helps you surround yourself with the right talent. My wish is that you dream big, lead with purpose and integrity, and master your craft. I hope—and believe—that *Startup CXO* will be a helpful companion for you on your company-building journey.

Good luck!

Scott Dorsey

Managing Partner – High Alpha

November 2020

Update for 2024 Edition

I was delighted to hear that Matt and his leadership team at Bolster are breaking out *Startup CXO* into a series of enhanced mini-books to cover the "big 5" functions in a startup -- Finance, HR, Sales, Marketing, and Product/Tech. Each of these mini books provides the reader with a streamlined view of the critical elements of a single leadership function in a startup and highlights some of the best thinking around how to hire and lead teams. This book is power-packed with actionable insights that will serve as a valuable resource as startup teams scale.

Enjoy!

Scott Dorsey

Managing Partner – High Alpha

August 2024

Introduction

Matt Blumberg

In 2020 we sold Return Path, a company we had grown from a startup to over 500 employees over two decades. I documented the CEO journey in *Startup CEO: A Field Guide to Scaling Up Your Business*, but after publishing *Startup CEO* I was left with the nagging feeling that it wasn't enough to only help CEOs excel, because starting and scaling a business is a collective effort. What about the other critical leadership functions that are needed to grow a company? If you're leading HR, or Finance, or Marketing, or any key function inside a startup, what resources are available to you? What should you be thinking about? What does "great" look like for your function? What challenges lurk around the corner as you scale your function that you might not be focused on today? What are your fellow executives focused on in their own departments, and how can you best work together? If you're a CEO who has never managed all these functions before, what should you be looking for when you hire and manage all these people? If you're an aspiring executive, from entry-level to manager to director, what do you need to think about as you grow your career and develop your skills? And if you're a Board client or investor, what scorecard or metrics are you using to ensure your companies and investments are achieving greatness?

A number of my Return Path colleagues and I founded Bolster shortly after exiting Return Path and we started thinking about a new book as a sequel or companion to *Startup CEO*. That was the origin of *Startup CXO: A Field Guide to Scaling Up Your Company's Critical Functions and Teams*. *Startup CXO* ended up being a "book of books," with eight separate, detailed sections, one for each major function inside a company. Each section was composed of several discrete short chapters outlining the key playbooks for each functional leadership role in the company. Because it covered CFOs, CMOs, CPOs, etc.--we landed on "Startup CXO" as the name. As a field guide, *Startup CXO* was massive—over 600 pages and 132 chapters and while we think the content is relevant to the entire leadership team, we recognize that a more focused book on each function is also something people need. The result is the book you have here, *Startup CTO: A Field Guide to Scaling up Your Company's Technology/Product Function*, which is written for the current or aspiring Chief Technology/Product Officer who wants to know how to scale their function, wants to know what "great" looks like, and wants to work effectively with other members of the organization. As an added benefit, this book is shorter, easier to carry, and cheaper.

While the content in this book is largely the same as *Startup CXO*, we updated it and added several chapters on "How to Hire a CPO," "How to Hire a CTO," and "How I Work With the Leadership Team." We also moved the chapter on Fractional work from *Startup CXO* to this book so that all of the relevant CTO/CPO information is in one book.

One major change we should note is a reflection of society: when we wrote *Startup CXO*, the pandemic was just underway and neither us nor anyone else could have predicted the impact globally, much less the drastic impact on startups and entrepreneurship. The impact of the pandemic on the world of work, in how business is conducted is well-known, from the great resignation to the permanence of remote work and hybrid models, but in the world of entrepreneurship the impact is less well-known. For example, in 2020 we wrote that "America's "startup revolution" continues to gather steam" and noted that there are "increasing numbers of venture capital investors, seed funds, and accelerators supporting increasing numbers of entrepreneurial ventures." Today the world has changed, and while startup activity is still quite high, we are seeing more down-rounds, re-pricings, and recaps as venture capitalists are de-risking their investments. We're seeing expanding deal timelines and a focus on governance and accountability. Founders are likely to be operating under a microscope with less leeway, and with more scrutiny on management accountability and structures ensuring performance-based compensation. What that means for today's founders is that they need to develop a great organization right out of the gate, and that's where *Startup CTO* will come in handy.

While there are a number of books in the marketplace about CEOs and leadership, and some about individual functional disciplines (lots of books on the topic of Sales, the topic of Product Development, and the like), there are very few books that are practical how-to guides for any individual function, and that is where this series of "mini books" can help guide startup and scaleup teams. Each book in this series will serve as a how-to guide for a given executive, and taken together, the series will be a good how-to guide for startup executive teams in general. The five books are:

Finance and Administration
People and Human Resources
Marketing
Sales
Product and Engineering

We are starting with these "big five," but we may come back later and add to the series with Customer Success, Privacy, Business Development, and Operations, the other sections of *Startup CXO.*

This book carries my name as its principal author, and although I'm writing parts of it and editing it, I'm not THE author, I'm AN author. Shawn Nussbaum has been CTO/CPO at Return Path and Bolster and he is the principal author and the person who has the experience, credibility, and expertise to share something of value with others in the Product organization. This material was also read and edited by additional CTO/CPOs we know.

One caveat. Although this book is being written by Shawn and me, it is not meant to be the Return Path story. We each have 20–30 years of experience working at multiple companies of different sizes and at different stages and in different sectors on which we are drawing. It's also not the story of Bolster, the new company that a number of us started during the pandemic in 2020. The book is based on our experience mostly in U.S.-based tech or tech-enabled services businesses, and more from the perspective of B2B than B2C, though inclusive of both. A few notes on language. We realize that not every leadership role in a startup is actually a "C"-level role. Sometimes the most senior person running a functional department is an SVP, a VP, a "head of," or even a Director or Manager. But Startup Functional Leader is a lousy title for a book. Regardless of title, we wrote with the most senior person responsible for the Product organization in mind. Another point on terminology is that we use the words startup and scaleup in the book without precise revenue-based or employee-count-based definitions, but you should assume that startups are smaller companies, whereas scaleups are ones that have already reached some meaningful level of critical mass. We also use terms like "executive team," "leadership team," "C-suite," and "executive committee" interchangeably to refer to a company's senior-most group of leaders. Finally, we frequently refer to the concept of an "operating system." I talked about this at length in my earlier book, *Startup CEO*, but basically, it means––whether for a person, a team, or a company––the collection of meeting and communication routines and operating practices that form the cadence of a team's work.

Although the book is focused on the CTO/CPO role, there are insights for others in an organization. So, if you're a CEO, you could gain some additional insight into why something is not working in your product organization––and understand how and what to change to create success in your Product team. I also have a "CEO-to-CEO Advice" section where I share my thoughts on what "great" looks like for the CTO/CPO, signs that your CTO/CPO isn't scaling, and how I engage with the CTO/CPO. I believe (and hope!) that CEOs, Board members, and investors can quickly get an overview and understanding of the CTO/CPO function by reading the "CEO-to-CEO Advice" chapter.

If you are a CTO/CPO or aspiring to become one, I hope this book speaks to you and inspires you in some way––that it's a playbook for something meaningful to you. If you're a CEO, maybe it will help you figure out who to hire or how to more effectively manage your CTO/CPO by telling you what "great" looks like for a CTO/CPO. If you're already a CTO/CPO in a startup, maybe it will help you focus on some aspect of your role you hadn't thought about yet. If you're an aspiring leader, maybe it will give you some insight into the kinds of steps you need to take in order to grow your career. Whichever persona you are, on behalf of me and Shawn, we hope you gain some insight, and we thank you for reading *Startup CTO: A Field Guide to Scaling up Your Company's Technology/Product Function.*

I. WELCOME TO THE EXECUTIVE TEAM

Matt Blumberg

Bolster Network

1

The Nature of a CXO's Role

I was struck by something as I read over the nearly complete manuscript of *Startup CXO* for the first time: each CXO believes that their part of the business is the most important part. And they make a compelling set of arguments:

Shawn: If you don't have a good product, you don't have a business.

Anita: If you don't have revenues, you don't have a business.

Ken: If you don't develop the ecosystem, you don't have a business.

Nick: If you don't generate market opportunities, you don't have a business.

George: If you don't create exceptional customer experiences, you don't have a business.

Cathy: If you don't recruit, train, and develop the right people, you don't have a business.

Jack: If you don't have the cash, you don't have a business.

Dennis: If you don't bake privacy in at the beginning, you don't have a business.

We had a debate years ago at a Return Path Board meeting as to whether we were a sales-driven business or a product-driven business—and more important, whether we should be one or the other.

Two of our Board members, both of whom I respect tremendously, were anchoring the different points of view, Scott Petry, on the product side, talking about how successful Apple was at getting customers to camp out overnight to be the first ones to buy the newest iThing; and Greg Sands, on the sales side, talking about how successful Oracle was at getting product into the hands of customers. I took a devil's advocate point of view in the conversation, true to our operating philosophy at Return Path, which was that HR/People was the most important function because we were a people-driven business.

So, who is right? Are the best companies sales-driven, product-driven, people-driven, or something else? Which of the CXO's functions is the most important? My answer is—they all are important, just in different ways, at different times, and in different combinations. While it's the CEO's job to balance the functions out—to figure out which lever to pull at which time, it's the CXO's job to be at the ready when their lever is pulled. And that gets to the important question of what the nature of a CXO role is, and why those roles can be tricky. CXOs have three principal jobs that they must keep in balance at all times, although there is a clear priority in my mind of the three jobs.

CXOs are first and foremost members of the company's Executive Team. They must, must, must put that team, understanding of the different functions, and the relationships on it at the top of their agenda. They shouldn't show up on the team only advocating for their own team. CEOs must insist on that behavior and mentality. Without it, a company simply can't function sustainably. This concept is one that we have always called the First Team concept, and it's articulated very eloquently by Patrick Lencioni in a number of his books, particularly in *The Five Dysfunctions of a Team* and *The Advantage*. As members of the Executive Team, all CXOs are accountable to each other for the success of the business as a whole and must partner with each other to achieve that success.

CXOs are also the head of their respective functional departments. They must carry the flag of their team and wave it proudly throughout the organization, especially when working with their teams. They are the functional role model, the functional mentor, and the functional decision-maker for the people on their functional team. To be an effective leader, they must be The Quintessential X (sales professional, engineer, marketer, etc.).

Finally, CXOs are company leaders. They are role models for company values. They should always be on alert for things that are going well or going poorly around them. Things that need attention or recognition. Situations that need calming down. Guests who are sitting unattended in the office lobby. Delivery people who need a check signed and who need to be tipped. Putting the new bottle of water onto the water cooler. You get the idea. Company leaders have the actual and moral authority to step outside of their departments and handle things as they need to be handled, regardless of which employees are involved.

Scaling a CTO/CPO

Congratulations, you just got promoted from Director of Product to Chief Product Officer! You're now in charge of a whole functional department, you now report to the CEO, you're now on the Executive Committee. You have a whole bunch of direct reports that either represent the team you used to lead or yesterday were your peers and you have now reached the pinnacle of your career in the Product organization. The only other ways to grow your career vertically are to lead your function at a larger and larger company, or to become a CEO. Wow!

That feeling of euphoria is wonderful. I remember having it when I worked at MovieFone and became the head of marketing and product management instead of just the "Internet guy." It definitely led to a nice celebratory night out in Manhattan with friends.

But then, the reality set in the next morning. Uh oh. I've never done this job before. Maybe I know how to do 25% of it. I'm only 26 years old. Is anyone going to respect me? I have so much to learn. Can I fake it? How on earth did I find myself here? This phenomenon is called the Imposter Syndrome, and it's totally normal. In fact, if you grow your career quickly, it would be weird not to have at least a touch of it.

The good news is, you're not the first person to be promoted to an executive role for the first time (and of course you're not the last, either). Every single executive, at any company, had their first executive role at some point. While there's some credence to the expression "fake it till you make it," there's a more methodical approach you can take to scaling yourself as a CTO/CPO—or if you're the CEO, to helping your new CTO/CPO scale. Think of the journey in three steps that can be taken in any order.

First, master the tactics. You need to understand all of the things that happen in your department. Some, you will know well because they're the ones you've done over time. Some you won't know at all. Make sure you do a complete inventory of the functional competencies for your role and all the roles reporting to you. Depending on how organized your company is with job descriptions and what's often known as a RACI (responsible-accountable-consulted-informed) analysis, this may be as easy as pulling something off the shelf and having a series of meetings with the people on your team to walk you through what they do. If your company isn't that organized, you may want to take the opportunity to proactively build that kind of functional competency/RACI list for everything in your team. That is no small exercise, but it's one that will pay back massive dividends. As one of my long-time colleagues, Anita Absey, has often reminded me, "What gets measured gets managed." I'd add to that: if you don't know something even exists, you can't begin to measure it, let alone manage it!

Second, form your strategic approach. Every single function in a company has tactical and transactional elements to it—and every single function can be ONLY tactical if you let it. That's the lowest common denominator. HR can be about benefits and payroll. Sales can be about pipeline management and closing deals. Marketing can be about blog posts and SEO. A transactional focus is especially true of corporate functions like HR and Finance, but it's true of all functions. But just as every function has its tactical elements that must be attended to, every function CAN be strategic. As you settle into your new role, and as you grow into the role of senior executive and learn the First Team lesson of putting the needs of the business before the needs of your department, you will be able to start thinking more holistically about the business and how your department fits into it, so when your CEO pulls the lever that indicates they need your team to step up and lead, to be strategic on some topic, you are ready. What does it mean to be strategic vs.

tactical? It's the difference between eating what's on your plate and planning out next week's menu. What are the ways in which the Product organization can produce competitive differentiation for the business? What are the frameworks that will guide your decision-making about resource allocation or prioritization? How can you best support the other departments in the company? Those are the kinds of things you need to master in step 2. As my colleague Dave Wilby once said about one of the teams he was managing, "We have to figure out how to be the nose, not the tail."

Finally, look around the corner to see what's next for you and for your team. Senior executives constantly need to be toggling between different execution and planning horizons. You need to make your goals this quarter, and to make them, you have to hit daily or weekly activity metrics and milestones. But what about next quarter? Or next year? Or what happens if your company doubles in size in the next six months and is set to double again? Start by revisiting that functional competency/RACI list from step 1 and stress-test every element of it. Ask yourself, What must be true of this line item when the company is twice its current size? While you have to develop and scale as a leader—with all that goes into that in terms of soft skills—the only way to scale yourself as a CPO is to understand what great looks like for your role at the next stage of the company's life, and make sure you don't get there after your company needs you to.

All three of these steps—mastering the tactics of your department, forming your strategic approach, and understanding what's next—are things you may be able to do on your own to a point. That said, they will all go more quickly and with a higher probability of success if you engage your CEO, your Head of HR, members of your Board, or outside mentors or coaches to assist you on your journey.

II. CHIEF TECHNOLOGY / PRODUCT OFFICER

Shawn Nussbaum and Matt Blumberg

Bolster Network

Chief Technology Officer and Chief Product Officer

Shawn Nussbaum

I never fully realized how much of an impact technical debt could have on a business until I found myself faced with an impossible challenge: I was responsible for a 100+ person product development team spread over three business units and two cities, supporting dozens of products on an aging platform, with a culture focused on maintenance and incremental change rather than on innovation. At the time, Return Path was a 16-year-old "startup" and I had been with them in leadership positions for seven years, so it wasn't like I was an expert brought in to change the product development organization––I had helped to create this problem. We were faced with slower growth and a changing market, and although we had a good business strategy to reorganize around our core competencies and we had overhauled our go-to-market machine with a compelling message, our Product Development organization was struggling under the load of a complex product set, an aging stack, and past decisions, and our product launches were often delayed, uncoordinated, and underwhelming.

Product and Engineering were in the hot seat and we were being asked tough questions from others in the company like, "Why does it take so long to get product out the door here?" and "Have we missed something over the years that has caused us to fall behind in product innovation?" Those were the questions that I was pondering myself as I looked at this challenge of getting the Product Development organization aligned with the rest of the business and firing on all cylinders. How do you change the culture of a large team and improve the velocity, while reinventing the underlying technology without pulling over to do it? That's the proverbial "change the engine while the car is running" problem.

I never would have predicted that I would have a 27-year career managing technology businesses nor that I would be writing a chapter in a book on how to create a great product development team. My family or friends might have predicted it, though. I grew up with two entrepreneurial grandfathers and learned the value of taking risks, working hard, and treating people well, and those traits are common to leaders of any team. I also liked to play around with computers as a kid and I remember finally getting bored with *Oregon Trail* on my Apple IIc and printing out the code and trying to figure out how everything worked. Through trial and error and a well-worn Apple BASIC book from the library, I created my own adventure game. In high school I was the "tech guy" who helped friends and family with their computers and networks. In college, I actually studied communication and music but was always programming on the side.

My first tech job was managing a small computer department for an insurance company and writing my first large business software program, an auto claims and billing system. I've been a hands-on technical contributor about 80% of my career, whether that's as an individual programmer or technical co-founder, and I have over 20 years of experience managing teams. I provide this short background because my journey is not all that different from other product and tech leaders. Many of us come from non-traditional backgrounds—without formal training in computer science or engineering—and I've found that we share common traits of being determined, hard-working, curious, and ready to dive in on any task or problem. My background is one part entrepreneurial, one part hands-on problem solver, and one part leader--and I'm most comfortable at the intersection of tech, business, and people.

The most formative parts of my career have all happened in startups, which I found to be places where you can work really hard with other people who want to create something. I've had three startup experiences: I worked in a startup that failed, a startup that scaled to $100mm and a successful exit, and a startup that went into zombie mode. As a startup, your favorite outcome is a successful exit, but the second favorite is an outright failure--so that you are free and clear to learn from the mistakes and go on to the next thing. The worst outcome is the zombie startup, the one where the company doesn't grow but it looks interesting enough to keep sucking you in for one more year to turn the crank and try to get it to be successful. In the zombie startup, I either felt like I had too much invested to leave or that success was right around the corner. So I stayed when I should have cut my losses.

Fortunately, you can learn lessons in all three cases and I want to share some stories, examples, and patterns I've used to run effective teams and drive technical and product strategy throughout this book.

The Product Development Leaders

Products are the lifeblood of a company; it's how customers experience and think about a company. A company's product is often synonymous with the brand—from Coca-Cola to Salesforce to Nike. And while a company can survive if some functions are ineffective, a company will never survive if their products are poorly designed, suffer from quality issues, or simply aren't useful. Getting your products right means getting the Product Development organization right, and that falls squarely on the shoulders of the Chief Technology Officer and the Chief Product Officer.

We're referring to Product Development quite broadly as the section responsible for designing, developing, and operating software products as a whole team. This means Engineering and Product Management as well as other functions in the product development process like data science, user experience, quality, infrastructure, and others. It is important to see this as one team since all these functions have a shared goal of building products that customers will use.

One of the challenges in Product Development is getting these separate functions to be one team, to communicate, collaborate, and to understand their roles/responsibilities so that they can create an effective product and customer experience. Part of your role as leader is to help make that partnership between the groups effective and, ultimately, make the partnership with the company effective.

The role of the product development leader changes depending on the stage of your growth. You might start with one generalist who manages everything "product" and add more functional leaders as you grow. outlines the core functions within product development and what they could look like at various stages of growth.

Startup Stage Responsibilities

Product

- Having a product leader is the most critical role for a company at the startup stage. The key responsibilities of the product leader are to determine what is going to get built, develop early adopters into paying customers, and get to product-market fit. In a raw startup the initial product leader could be a technical co-founder with deep product experience and knowledge of the business/industry. Or it could be the CEO paired with a strong engineer who is building the first version of the product.

Engineering

- In the early stage, the technical cofounder/CTO is a hands-on engineer responsible for building the minimum viable product (MVP) and the initial engineering team. They need to define the initial technical choices for the business, balancing pragmatism and the need to be lean and get to early product-market fit, with enough of a long-term technical strategy not to be buried in technical debt as the business scales. This individual could be a more experienced leader who is also responsible for product management in the early days, or a strong technical contributor paired with a product leader.

Design/UX

- The role of a product designer is also critical at the startup stage, and they work closely with the product manager to ensure that the product is successful—specifically the interaction between the customer and the product and the usability of the product. They are responsible for product discovery, UX, building UI mock-ups and prototypes, and user testing. An early-stage company will likely have Product Design report into the head of Product instead of a dedicated leader of UX.

Data/Analytics

- Data includes engineers responsible for collecting and processing data and data analysts/scientists responsible for extracting meaning from data. Data is increasingly becoming core to businesses—not just for decision making, but as part of the product, or it is the actual product. Depending on the business, the early Data team could be a core strategic function, or it could be one or more analysts who report to the Head of Engineering initially.

Growth Stage Responsibilities

Product

- As the business grows, Product Development and Technology Development start to become more independent from each other (but still highly collaborative). Product leadership is now splitting features across multiple teams and needs to balance maintenance, growth, and innovation across the product. While there are individual product managers at this stage, they still might report up to one business leader that is responsible for Product Development as a whole.

Engineering

- In the growth stage, the focus is on scaling the initial team, enhancing the early product, and becoming more efficient. Hiring and team composition start to become more specialized instead of the focus on generalists that were part of the initial company. Multiple teams are built to take on parts of the product and focus on key technical areas, so it is important to build front-line leaders and an effective project/process framework to manage and measure work. While there are distinct front-line leaders in Engineering at this stage, they still might report up to one business leader that is responsible for Product Development as a whole. If your initial engineering leader was a strong individual contributor, you should be hiring a technical leader to drive strategy across the organization.

Design/UX

- Depending on the complexity of the product and number of product lines, you will be scaling the product design team and likely looking for a dedicated leader for this function, or at least a team lead. One area that becomes critical at this stage is having consistency or a style guide across multiple product lines. Structuring this team to be able to pair with a Product Manager for day-to-day work, but also have a functional design review process can help balance this.

Data/Analytics

- At the growth stage, the data leader is responsible for scaling the team and collaborating with the rest of the product development functions. A key decision that often needs to be made at this point is whether to structure this team as more of a service bureau or embedded in the product teams and navigating the tradeoffs of each approach.

Mature Stage Responsibilities

Product

- It is important at this scale to have a dedicated product leader who owns the overall product strategy and roadmap across the business and is effective at delegating strategy ownership to the individual product managers and collating and communicating those strategies across the business and externally. A core responsibility as the Head of Product is to build a great team of product managers and set the product culture for the organization.

Engineering

- It is important at this scale to have a dedicated engineering leader who owns technical strategy and has dedicated leaders owning key functions within engineering (infrastructure, quality, etc.). The engineering leader is responsible for communicating and getting buy-in to the strategy/philosophy for technical direction and development practices and should be able to articulate and defend a business plan on how technology can be used as a force-multiplier for the business to drive innovation or efficiency as the business grows.

Design/UX

- At this scale, the product design team will generally have a dedicated leader and report to the C-level product leader.

Data/Analytics

- At this scale, the data team will generally have a dedicated leader and report to the C-level product or technical leader, or in some cases be a C-level role directly (if data is the product).

———

While a company might start out with one leader responsible for Product Development as a whole, it is important to understand that there is value to having dedicated owners of the Product and Engineering functions. Building a great product requires managing tradeoffs between the functionality and value of something versus what is feasible. Often what the business needs and what Engineering needs can be opposite from each other, and this creates a natural tension that is good and forces tradeoffs and collaboration that can result in better products. World-class product companies have become good at managing this push/pull between Product Management and Engineering. It is important to cultivate managing this tension somewhere in the organization even at the early stage. It doesn't have to be between two C-level leaders over Product and Engineering initially; it could be just between a strong Product Manager and a Technical Lead.

One other point about technology leaders: There seems to be a lot of opinions about the differences between Chief Technology Officer (CTO) and VP of Engineering and we've seen organizations debate and cargo cult this for our entire careers. We've heard, for example, "the CTO is always the founding technical engineer and should always be the CTO (no matter if they can't manage their way out of a paper bag)," or "the CTO has to be the most technical person in the company," or "the VP of Engineering doesn't have to be deep technically because they are just a people manager and makes sure the trains run on time, and they should always report to the CTO," and on and on. The reality is that the most senior person who is responsible for the technical strategy for a company should be a leader. They should be the person who can handle the responsibilities of this role and at the size/stage of the company.

Let's break that down. They need to be a leader, not the strongest programmer at the company. They need to be able to communicate deep technical details to internal and external business stakeholders. They need to be able to grow a leadership team and effectively manage people. They need to be a delivery manager and make sure that the work of designing, building, delivering, and managing the product gets done efficiently and effectively. And, maybe the key part: they need to understand how to use technology as a strategic asset to help the business succeed, and, by that we mean, they are in the room when the big business decisions get made. The technology leader can't let the team just be the technical arm of a company that is handed specifications to go build. They have to ensure that Product Development is integral to the business. That is, they need to help set the product vision and strategy and execute Product Development across the organization in collaboration with internal and external business stakeholders.

Not every technical leader fits the bill, and not every technical leader is competent across all the stages of growth. The upstart hacker/CTO may be fine for building the minimum viable product (MVP) and getting the company to Series A, but if that's what you have, you should look for developing leadership around this person if you plan to scale anywhere important. The IT leader who spent their career at large companies might be good in a middle management job with a lot of structure and great at managing products in maintenance mode, but if your scaleup business has a deep technical product and a strategic roadmap that requires technical integration with partners, they will soon be out of their depth around driving technical vision and strategy.

What I Look For in a Product Development Leader

When I started my career as a product manager, the role of Chief Product Officer didn't even exist. My PM group oscillated between reporting up to the VP of Engineering or the VP of Marketing, depending on the latest powerplay or recommendation from "the consultants." But since those early days the Product function has become more influential and today Product is the nexus between all parts of the business—operational, technical, and go-to-market.

With that increased influence and dependency between product and other critical functions, the organizational structure of most companies, especially tech companies, has changed. Today it's common to have the product management function report up to a Chief Product Officer. That CPO typically reports to (or will report to) the CEO, and sits at the executive table next to the CTO and the CMO.

CPOs are invariably senior technical leaders but having the title "CPO" doesn't necessarily reduce conflict or confusion with other technical leadership positions. Who is responsible for the product, the CPO or the CTO? Who do employees need to consult or inform on decisions related to product, the CPO or the CTO? Confusion on the role of the CPO is rampant in many companies and there have been a number of wide-ranging and informative blog posts trying to differentiate the role of the CPO from the CTO. One common theme on the difference between the CPO and the CTO is that the CPO should be responsible for the "why" a company invests in a particular product, leaving the "how" to the technical teams.

While this is a good model for differentiating the roles, I've seen too often that CPOs are assessed and performance-reviewed based on their raw technical chops rather than their ability to assess a market opportunity and rally the organization behind the cause.

CPOs are typically classically trained engineers who have expanded their skills beyond technology and product development into business-related issues. But even with the addition of business acumen, I have seen many CPOs revert to their comfort zone. For example, where the ambiguity of the market obscures clear answers, CPOs may hesitate, delay decisions, or ask for more data; but where issues are more concrete, say, in selecting a new tech stack, CPOs will become highly engaged, debate issues, and influence the choice.

It's not just CPOs themselves who struggle with the "why" of product; non-technical people who evaluate CPO candidates or peer performance reviewers also place a greater, asymmetric weight on the technical assertiveness of the CPO. In my opinion, that's the wrong measure.

Clearly, the CPO needs to understand the technical aspects of the product and its place in the market—that's the baseline, the bare minimum that a CPO ought to know. Another big "why" the CPO needs to understand is "why are customers buying (or not buying) our solution?" The answer to this question is more difficult to figure out. The CPO needs to have enough business sense to understand market white spaces, enough technical expertise to understand technical trends and direction shifts, and enough social media knowledge to understand the role of analysts, influencers, and societal trends impacting why customers buy or don't buy a solution. Mapping what Engineering can develop to what the customer will buy requires soup-to-nuts understanding and expertise, not just familiarity with the latest SDLC model or development stack. The intersection of social, technical, and market forces on consumer behavior is where the most fertile answers are found, but this is the area fraught with ambiguity and uncertainty. It is the place where CPOs need to spend their time, but the place many deeply technical people try to avoid.

I look at the CPO as being an emotional leader in the company more than a technical leader. Of course, the CPO needs significant technical chops to be credible and to focus the product development efforts. But the full measure of their emotional leadership capabilities needs to be applied to rallying the organization behind the initiative. The "why" needs to resonate with each internal team. Why should Finance care? Why will HR benefit? Why will differentiation from competitors help Sales and Marketing improve their performance?

Technical chops are table stakes for a CPO. But good CPOs are evangelists, and with great CPOs, you might never even know they come from a technical background.

Scott Petry, *Cofounder and CEO, Authentic8*

5

Product Development Culture

Good culture is a strategic advantage for a business and this is the key in the product development organization too, because everything else hangs off of your culture. Your ability to create remarkable products is a lot more likely if you have a culture that embraces innovation and creativity. Your ability to balance the team between pragmatism proportional to the business while hitting real outcomes (not just output) is accelerated with a good culture. Your ability to adapt and change as the company grows is a direct result of the culture you create.

While the product development team benefits from the overall company culture, it is a distinct subculture within a business and it's important to understand those differences and cultivate the culture you need if you want an effective product development organization. The first things to get right about your culture is exactly how you'll fit within the larger company.

The product development team is not just the execution-arm for the company. They own the roadmap and they're the ones shaping the product to have the biggest impact on customers. You can't do this alone and you'll need to cultivate a collaborative relationship with other functions like Sales and Marketing to understand their strategies. It's not uncommon to get requests from the business to experiment on things, but I'd suggest that you keep this in perspective because you'll have your own needs and requirements to manage innovation, technical debt, and product lifecycle.

Another thing to do to ensure that the culture of the product development team is focused on the right activities is to create space so that the team is a product group, not a project group. Some companies still see and treat product development as if it were similar to manufacturing where processes are repetitive and outcomes are reasonably predictable. If you try to utilize a product development team like you would a team in a manufacturing facility, you'll set the team up for failure. A product development team runs into many problems that are unpredictable and your teams will need time to experiment and learn through discovery and feedback from users.

Types of Development Cultures

We've experienced three different types of development cultures and only one of them is what you'd want to strive for. One development culture is what we call an "over-engineering" style. In this culture, the leadership and engineers want to solve everything with engineering and, although it can be good, the cumulative engineering investment over time is far greater than what the business needs at that stage of growth. The result is that you have disproportionately invested too much in engineering relative to the business need. You built a Mercedes when what the customer really needs is a bicycle. One exception to this is if you are building safety-critical systems (avionics, pacemakers, self-driving cars, etc.) and need to over-engineer—especially on quality.

Companies that over-invest in engineering are often trying to create a culture that attracts great engineers who want to solve difficult, complex, or interesting engineering problems. What you really need to create a great development culture are engineers who want to solve business problems with engineering. We've seen companies create the over-engineering approach, thinking that they could out-guess where the business is going and they end up over-optimizing before the business gets there. Most of the time this guesswork is just completely divorced from any business reality and what you have is a group of engineers, isolated from the market and customers, thinking about their own problems, or their pride in work or modeling things after what Google or other successful high-profile companies do.

Another development culture is what we call an "under-engineering" style. In this approach, companies disproportionately invest too little in engineering relative to the business need. This can start out noble and appropriately pragmatic which is what most raw startups should do. But, if left unchecked, the product development team stays overly pragmatic and scrappy too long and they become reactive and in service to the business instead of in partnership with the business. Chapter 3 covers this problem in detail.

Good-enough solutions sometimes lag behind the business and then you'll need more of a step-function to catch up. The problem is, if you operate with an under-engineering, scrappy style, you'll always be in crisis mode, your team will be overworked, and morale will plummet. We've seen the under-engineering model play out in a couple of ways. One way is that the business and the product development organization are misaligned and not communicating on where the business is going and what role product and technology play in that overall strategy. This can happen because there's a weak product development leader, or it could happen because there's a really strong business leader who doesn't understand the cost of cutting corners. Or this can happen because a product development leader or engineering team is disconnected from the business and values an overly scrappy approach technically without understanding the real cost of unchecked technical debt.

The third development culture that we've seen, and the one we'd recommend, is what we call a "proportional approach." In this model you invest proportionally in Engineering relative to the business need. You'll need a strong vision on technology being a strategic advantage to make it work. The result will be that your product development team will be highly aligned with the business and in lock-step with the product organization. Sometimes you may even be able to get ahead of the business and experiment to drive innovation, but in this model your experimenting will be focused on things that the market needs, not just innovation to be innovating. The figure below presents the types of development culture.

Types of Development Culture

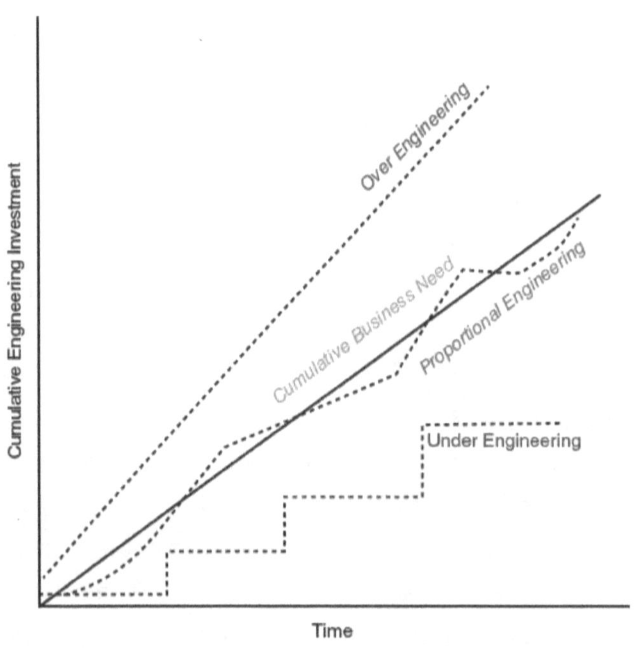

6

Technical Strategy

Proportional Engineering Investment and Managing Technical Debt

As a product or technology leader at a startup, you have an opportunity to build the first version of the product, grow the team, and set the culture and strategy for your organization. That's a great and humbling responsibility. We started this Part on Product Development by introducing a challenge that Return Path was facing around getting the product development organization aligned with the rest of the business and firing on all cylinders again. Startups don't begin with those types of problems but it's important to look at the impact that decisions have on a fast-growing company and learn from those lessons. No one will get their product, infrastructure, or culture right—even when they have the opportunity to start it from scratch. However, being intentional about where you want to go and diligent about changing things that break—or end up being wrong—is the key to long-term success. You can't avoid technical debt as you grow, but you can be intentional about amortizing it as you go so that it doesn't compound and negatively impact innovation and velocity.

So, how did Return Path get there, with a big pile of technical debt? We held on to an approach that worked really well as a startup and then we didn't change it as the company grew, as markets evolved, as technology choices broadened, or as new competitors emerged. We didn't invest proportionally.

When you're working in maintenance and incremental improvement modes, you can easily lose sight of the fact that healthy companies grow and change—quickly. The product development organization that you start with has to also continue to adapt and support (and sometimes get ahead of) the business as it grows. As a Product or Engineering leader, you'll need to get comfortable with the idea that your current philosophies and approach will be wrong at some point and you will be continually challenged to be the leader that the organization needs at that stage of its growth.

For our product development team we had two things working against us that slowed us down and made it difficult for us to generate the velocity and innovation that we needed: unaddressed technical debt and complexity.

Like many startups, our founders were technical and pragmatic and they had a scrappy approach to building products and a business. It's actually what attracted me (Shawn) to Return Path in the first place, since the engineers weren't just focused on solving technical problems but were interested in solving bigger picture business issues. But while the scrappy, pragmatic approach that we had as a startup helped us survive, we didn't have a strategy or the time to manage around it.

There's a saying that, "In engineering, you pay for it now or later, but you always pay for it." As a startup, we were scrappy and, on the positive side, that meant that we were fast, efficient, practical, did prototypes, and hit the outcome without caring as much for the methods used to do it. But being scrappy also meant that we took shortcuts, made temporary fixes, were short-term thinkers, and had scalability issues. While the leaders at Return Path knew how to balance scrappy with areas that needed more rigor, that same thinking didn't always translate to the teams doing the work. Teams often cited "scrappy" as an excuse to cut corners and borrow too much technical debt to hit a goal or just get something out the door. Those decisions created a culture and a foundation that later became an issue when we put stress on the system to move faster and innovate.

Another aspect of unaddressed technical debt is the real operational cost of maintaining active products. Business and product development leaders are generally good at understanding and measuring the time and cost of new product development, like having a team of six work for six months to accomplish X. What is less understood—or is taken for granted—is what it takes to operate a product that is in market. This is especially true at companies that are early stage, high growth, or have limited resources. We're not talking about core products that are undergoing active development because those are typically staffed with full teams that are balancing new development and ongoing maintenance. We're referring to products that are still supported in the market but don't have large ongoing development and are more in maintenance mode—on the shelf.

There are at least three components of operational costs to support products that are actively in the market but are not core:

- **Ongoing maintenance and bug fixes.** This is the main area that leaders know about and consider when keeping a product active but on the shelf. Operational costs include monitoring, production support, and bug fixes.

- **Incremental development.** This is also understood well by most product development leaders, but it's unlikely to be accounted for from a time and budget standpoint. Most products that are on the shelf might not have a team assigned to operate them; instead, those products are just being monitored by another team or a dedicated engineering support team. But even a product on the shelf will at some point need an incremental update to support a marketing launch or a message or visual change. Any change usually requires people who can dive back into a product and learn about the product and make whatever changes are necessary. In theory, it sounds easy to just throw more people at it, but it can be more challenging than it sounds, depending on the change and the challenges with older technology and finding people to go deep on it. Incremental changes also can introduce additional bugs or support requirements that make it harder for the product to just be put back on the shelf when the incremental change is made.

- **Technical updates.** This third area is often overlooked by business leaders and can sometimes be overlooked even by technical leaders if they aren't paying attention to their technical debt or products on the shelf. If big changes happen in technology, security, and privacy that affect the platform, then all of the products—not just the core products—are affected. For instance, if the business moves from a data center to the cloud, then every product has to be updated to support containerization; if a data feed or data processing platform changes, then every product has to be updated to consume from this new service; if the business has to adopt a new privacy law or audit protocol, then every product has to be updated. When you have multiple products in maintenance mode on the shelf, this last type of ongoing maintenance is a killer and introduces a lot of thrash and distraction into the development process—pulling teams apart to work on old products that need to be reworked to support these deep platform changes. And when old products haven't been refactored or updated recently, it takes time and expertise to change them. In addition, often there is no time to refactor or rewrite them, so ad-hoc changes are made and bugs or scaling issues are introduced.

How do you manage the challenges of shelf products? Ideally, you would have dedicated teams for each product that is active and in market, but smaller, scrappier companies that are moving fast and trying out different solutions to get to product-market-fit are often not staffed to dedicate people this way. You could have a dedicated maintenance team that manages all of the on-the-shelf products, but that solution is challenging because it is seen as maintenance work and doesn't attract senior engineers and what you really need, especially with larger platform changes I mentioned above, are senior engineers with deep familiarity with those products to make changes. You could have each active product development team take on a set of on-the-shelf products, but be prepared for that team's velocity to slow down as they have to move six things forward an inch at a time instead of moving one thing forward six inches at a time. It also eats into team morale and creates a large set of technology requirements for that team to be experts in.

There are no really good answers when it comes to managing a large set of on-the-shelf-products, but there are a couple of best practices. The best strategy is to prevent a company from getting in too much of a hole by having clear ownership and strong product lifecycle management. Be diligent about measuring and articulating the real cost of operating things and aggressive about killing things even if it impacts ongoing revenue. Limit the number of technologies (as much as you can) and be vigilant about keeping products up to date technically so you don't have big catch-up moments.

While unaddressed technical debt was a contributing factor to our product development challenges at Return Path, the other factor was complexity. We had multiple businesses with a vast number of technologies in use. Some of the technology issues came from a dozen acquisitions over the years, and we didn't properly address how those would be managed long-term. And some technology issues came from our approach where each dedicated product team made its own technical decisions as long as they owned them. That independence afforded to the technical team worked really well in the early stages of our growth because we had several large teams responsible for a few key products. As the company grew and developed many products and as people moved between teams, our approach wasn't that great. Sure, from a talent standpoint, we had our experts distributed to the individual product teams and we had a few central teams that were responsible for operations, support, and platforms. But the central teams were staffed by mid- to junior engineers, and they weren't seen as important as the product teams. We couldn't easily standardize or create common tools because of the complexity of each individual team and because of the inexperience of the central teams.

After looking deeply at our current reality this is what we found: Not every team had legacy systems they were dealing with, some were already in the cloud, up to date, had high business alignment, no distractions and great velocity. But the teams differed enough that it slowed down the company. A bigger problem was that with many products (and a large number of them on the shelf), coupled with years of putting off technical upgrades, and lower morale with people having too many technologies to be experts in, we had a culture where we dragged everything forward and continued to take shortcuts on top of shortcuts. And without us realizing, "scrappy" had become "crappy." One team had 30 products that were important to the business with a team of 30 engineers responsible for them, and this was the team we expected to innovate and drive high velocity changes to the business.

Sometimes when you are faced with a velocity challenge, you can just add more engineers and power through—and that works if your systems and processes can support moving faster with quality and efficiency. At Return Path, we didn't have that and we were dealing with a perfect storm of people, process, and technology issues that were gumming up the works.

We started by setting three big priorities that needed to change to get the product leadership team and development team aligned:

- **Talent.** First, we needed to step up and lead. We needed to be driving the technical and product strategy for the business and not just reacting to things or building whatever was asked of us without considering the costs. We got traction on this by having technical conversations and partnering with the business on decisions.

- **Team.** Within the product development team we started driving standards/practices across product development so that everyone was aligned and rowing in the same direction. We started a mentorship and onboarding process for new engineers so that they could become productive sooner. And we created an Architecture Council to get the senior-level engineers involved and working on core issues and not just sequestered on their individual product teams.

- **Tooling.** We needed to be more efficient and stop using different technologies on each team so we created an engineering efficiency/tooling team to drive DevOps patterns, automation, and central tools and services that every team could benefit from. If done well, using a few really good engineers in a centralized team like this can be a force-multiplier across the organization.

- **Technology.** The third priority was around modernizing our aging systems. By taking an iterative approach, we slowly moved data centers to the cloud, servers to containers, scheduled jobs to services and workflows, data processing from large batch processes to streaming analytics.

It wasn't a fast or easy change to implement in the product development organization, but a nice side effect of prioritizing teams, tooling, and technology was that we were able to hire more early-career engineers on product teams because they could learn the stack quickly and not have the complexity that existed in each team before. Another benefit was that people could move between teams and still be able to use the same technology, processes, standards, and practices that they learned on the first team.

Getting the product development organization aligned behind all these changes wasn't difficult philosophically because engineers are fairly motivated around good practices and newer technologies. The main pain points were around organizing the people and the work to balance the technical debt work with ongoing maintenance and new feature development. We also had a small group of good engineers who unfortunately decided to leave the organization during this change because they either saw this change as an indictment on them being too scrappy or they just had a different philosophy around engineering. So, that was a bummer.

The biggest challenge in any large technical refactor will always be how to communicate it to the Board, the CEO, and your peers on the executive team. We needed to get their support to make these changes in the first place, and after getting the support, we had to manage the timeline and expectations during the journey.

You'd think, given how the product development organization was widely perceived to be the "problem," that the Board, the CEO, and executive team would be super-supportive of our strategic plan to make the product organization fast and innovative, but a perceived need is not enough to move the needle. After all, we were the ones responsible for the situation we were in. So we created a story and used data to drive home the point that without a dramatic change in the product development organization, we would be unable to overcome our situation and get back on track for high growth.

The first part of the story presented our current reality of unaddressed technical debt and overly complex systems (lots of them!) for the type and stage of our business. It's important, especially if you're making a big change, to make sure that everyone else sees what you see and agrees that it's actually a problem. The second part of the story captured and presented our challenges with data, quantified in a way that would make it impossible for a reasonable person to disagree with our plan.

Two artifacts really helped drive our point home. The first artifact was a table listing the full product development team members with the category of work that they spent time on. That table cross-referenced that time spent working with the terms "tomorrow, today, and yesterday." Every healthy product has Today and Tomorrow work. Today is the cost of maintaining a product, making incremental changes, and refactoring the technology stack to stay up to date, balancing incurring technical debt with paying it off. Tomorrow work includes the active development to add functionality and continue to evolve the product. Older systems in maintenance-only mode might just have Today work. At Return Path we had Yesterday work as well, and that's not good. We had team members spending time dealing with old systems that were important to the business but not cared for actively by a team. Even worse, these systems generated all types of effort that the business wasn't aware of. When we first generated the table, we had 30% of our team working on Yesterday, 60% on Today, and 10% on Tomorrow. That was an eye opener! We had a visual story of why we couldn't innovate and move faster.

The second artifact was a stacked area chart that showed the allocation of engineers across product lines looking back four years along with release milestones. It showed where the business put its focus and where some of the teams were running slower or missing outcomes because they had so much drag. We added 18 months of forward-looking details that included an investment in Yesterday work to illustrate the impact and timeline of digging out of the hole.

These two artifacts, along with the narrative around unaddressed technical debt and complexity, were used to tell the story to the Board, the CEO, executive team, and everybody in the company. We also used the data on time spent and the categories of Today, Tomorrow, and Yesterday to update everyone on our progress as we went along. The metrics (% of engineers on Today/Tomorrow vs. Yesterday) became part of my KPIs as we embarked on the journey to "Slow Down to Speed Up." Ultimately we were able to finish that work and move the product team back to a high velocity, efficient, and effective team that was focused again on Today and Tomorrow work.

7

Shifting to a New Development Culture

Y ou don't want to wait to shift your development culture until your technical debt is so high that you're in a big hole, like we were at Return Path. I (Shawn) can tell you from first-hand experience that being the part of the business holding everyone back and having all the fingers pointed at you is not a good place to be. But what can you do that will actually change your development culture? Fortunately, there are steps you can take to alter your development culture and they don't have to be dramatic—you just have to be consistent in your approach. One of the best examples of changing a culture is from Ed Catmull's (2014) book, *Creativity, Inc*, where he tells the story of Pixar. Catmull highlights that the right leadership, transparency, and candor can foster a great culture and lead to innovative results. In 2006, Disney acquired Pixar not only for the technology and talent, but to take the Pixar culture to Disney. At the time of the merger, Disney was in a 16-year trough since their last number 1 hit. They had a lousy work environment, a leadership imbalance that diminished creativity, filmmakers who had lost their voice and were afraid of pouring their hearts into something that wouldn't succeed. They saw themselves as hired guns, not owners of high-quality films, and they weren't empowered to fix what was broken. In short, they were playing it safe and being a utility. The Pixar culture of innovation, candor, freedom, and change was brought into Disney and four years later Disney released *Tangled*. It became the second highest grossing film from Disney Animation ever, after the *Lion King* 16 years earlier. The key was that the studio was still populated by most of the same people from before. What changed was that the leaders applied Pixar's principles to a dysfunctional culture and team and changed them—unleashing their creative potential.

Developing products, like making a film, is an inherently creative process and creating requires making thousands of small decisions that result in a unique outcome. Some companies approach product development as a utility: functional, practical, pragmatic, do what's expected, no frills, no drama, don't piss people off—just get it done. And for certain products and companies that works and is good enough. But if the key goals of a product are to inspire, solve a problem, be fun to use, be efficient, and amaze the users of it, then the people creating that product have to be innovators, creators, and be deeply empathetic about their users. Empathy and usefulness are the keys to remarkable products. Like Pixar, if you want to create an environment that is able to harness innovation and creativity, you have to do more than have a culture that makes people feel valued—you have to create an environment that makes them valuable to the business and to make that happen, you'll have to connect the dots from the work your team does to how it impacts a customer or drives a sale. You have to give people freedom to fail and make mistakes. You have to be candid/transparent with them and give them the data to make decisions. And, you have to let them have real ownership over something.

Setting the right set of values is important in changing a culture. With the under-engineering culture we had a value that said, "Focus on achieving the outcome, not the methods used to achieve the outcome" and that is what we delivered—the outcome, and nothing more. We didn't think much about the technical choices we were making, and we weren't intentional about the product lifecycle. You can't just keep making products and putting them in market without understanding the ongoing cost of operating them (or helping the business understand that). Building a partnership between Product Development and the business and investing proportionally in engineering was the key to maximizing our effectiveness.

Here are the Product Development team values we ended up with at Return Path to drive the type of culture we wanted:

- **Be effective.** The business outcome matters. Our number one job is to create value for the business—have a bias for action.

- **Be intentional.** Think about the methods behind a problem; think end-to-end; build something that works for today but scales for tomorrow; use data to learn and inform decisions.

- **Be efficient.** Creativity is important, but don't waste time; try something and learn quickly; don't reinvent the wheel; use patterns and tools.

- **Be awesome.** Build stuff that is awesome and works—we care about quality and driving technical innovation in our products and platforms.

- **Be iterative.** Take an incremental and proportional step to achieve the business outcome based on learnings.

- **Be collaborative.** Seek counsel from peers and contribute your knowledge.

Things to Consider

- Rewriting and migrating big systems are risky and time-consuming. The better alternative to a complete rebuild is to slowly and systematically take over the old application. You gain immediate benefits and reduce risk. Martin Fowler calls this the "Strangler Pattern," and a blog post of his contains a great metaphor of strangler vines around a tree that is a perfect visual for this work.

- Creating an Architecture Council with senior-level engineers across the organization has multiple benefits for engineers and the company. It provides a career path for engineers; it gives teams a framework for making decisions instead of relying on the CTO to make all decisions; and it allows the Product organization to coordinate and work on overarching initiatives across the company instead of just on individual product teams.

- Hackathons can be a good way to foster collaboration and innovation across the company. We ran hackathons a couple times a year and encouraged employees outside of Product Development to join teams, providing a broad range of ideas and experiences. Some great product ideas came out of this and it set a culture of creativity and experimentation.

8

Starting Things

As mentioned before, if you have the opportunity to start an idea and a company from scratch, it's a great and humbling experience. You get to solve a problem for a customer in a specific way and get them to pay you for that solution. You get to build a team and set a culture, and you get to pick the technology and build the product that will change the world—or at least you hope for all that!

This chapter outlines a few of the practices that we used when starting something from scratch.

Startups face two initial challenges before they can shift to growth mode. The first challenge is to define their idea (that will become a product) and determine if it addresses a problem that's worth solving. The second challenge is to build the first version of that product and get to product/market fit, which is the moment where customers are paying for your product and you are retaining them.

If this is a raw startup, then you are creating a product and a company at the same time. We like to use Ash Maurya's Lean Canvas, from his (2012) startup book *Running Lean*, to document the initial business plan. The Lean Canvas is a one-page business model template that is simple and quick to use to capture the building blocks of your business model and then systematically test each element until the idea is sufficiently validated or de-risked to continue. For defining and validating the idea, you have to get out and talk to potential customers to understand if they have this problem, how they are solving it today, and if they care enough about you solving it for them. Ash Maurya has a great framework in *Running Lean* that I like to use to do structured problem interviews with customers.

Here are a few things to keep in mind when validating an early idea and talking to potential customers:

- Problem interviews are mostly about setting the context and then listening to customers. Do they have this problem? How do they solve this today? Is there a possible competing product that they are using to solve this problem?

- Is this problem a must have (pain killer) or a nice to have (vitamin)?

- The bigger the pain point for a customer, the more likely you have found an early adopter, especially if they have hacked their own solution to solving this problem.

- Pay attention to anything that holds a customer back from moving to a new solution or anything that prevents them from using a solution.

- Listen to what customers say, but more importantly, watch what they do. When you build a product, you have to balance listening *to* customers with innovating *for* them. Pay attention to the problem they have, not necessarily their specific idea about how you should solve it.

- Make sure you are aligned with the benefit or outcome the customer is looking for and not some intermediate solution or experience. The old business school adage is that "people don't want quarter-inch drill bits, they want quarter-inch holes."

Once you have determined that you have a problem worth solving, you can then move on to the second challenge which is to build the first version of your product. This phase isn't a single process to build and launch the product, but rather an iterative process of continuously refining your product until you achieve product/market fit and are ready to optimize and scale your business.

In our startup experience, getting to product/market fit is the hardest part. There is something special about an idea in your head that always initially gets worse when you start to build a product. Early versions of a product are intentionally minimal, with rough user interfaces (UI) and limited functionality, but early versions create a gap between the end state you envision in your head and what you see being developed. You'll eventually (hopefully) close this gap as you continue to iterate and complete the product, but just starting can be a big challenge. The best remedy for this stage is to just keep moving (even if the direction doesn't feel right) because you learn by moving and you incorporate that learning to make the product better.

Having a framework or methodology is useful for getting into this validated learning loop. We like to use the Build-Measure-Learn loop that is described in *The Lean Startup* by Eric Ries (2011). It relies on validated learning as the key unit of progress with the goal to eliminate uncertainty (fail fast) and narrow down the core problem and solution and then iteratively build out the minimum viable product (MVP).

So, now we have a high-level plan in our Lean Canvas and a feedback loop framework to guide our experiments to iteratively build something, test it, learn, and build something else. The missing piece is a project management tool for managing the details. Typically, something like Trello (at the early stage) and then something robust like Jira (as the company gets bigger) work well. The problem is that the project tool is flat and is just a prioritized list of cards to work on. Something is missing in between the Lean Canvas and Trello. That's where Story Maps fit in. Story Maps were created by Jeff Patton (2014) and are two-dimensional maps that contain "big stories" or user activities across the top and then have progressive levels of detail on the vertical axis to define specific cards that relate to that user action. Story Maps are incredibly useful to define the outcomes that users want to accomplish with your product—kind of like a living requirements document about the product that you are finalizing. The big stories at the top (which are basically "epics") are not prioritized and don't change as much, but the stories under them are prioritized and are part of various release swim lanes to organize and plan the work.

Here are a few things to keep in mind when iterating on your MVP and getting to product/market fit:

- MVP is really about the minimum functionality that you need to show to validate learning. Some people refer to the "P" in MVP as "prototype" instead of "product" to make this point. Sometimes you don't need much more than a user interface mock-up to validate an idea and then you can start building the product.

- When you start building early versions of the product, it is useful to think about each release as a complete working product—albeit limited. For example, if the goal is to end up with a car, it is more useful releasing a skateboard first, followed by a bicycle, and finally a car. If you are iterating on a car and your first version is a car with one wheel followed by a car with two wheels, it isn't useful to anyone.

- Be prepared to change direction or pivot many times in your validated learning loop before settling on a version that you want to build a product around. Pivot before getting to product/market fit and then optimize after that.

As a technology leader, one of your key responsibilities in the early stage is choosing the technology, building the MVP, and delivering the first version of the product. Here are some thoughts about technical choices:

- At the early stage it is all about supporting validated learning. This usually means that where possible you should use UI mocks, simple prototypes, or simple web landing pages in your Build-Measure-Learn loop.

- There are a number of services that you can use to build fully functional applications quickly. For instance, a combination of Webflow, Zapier, and Airtable can be used to quickly spin up a templated web application with integrations to most SaaS services and an experimental data model.

- As you move from prototype to building the application, you can get many benefits from using cloud providers. For example, if you use managed services on a cloud provider for the database, queues, containers, logging, and deployment then you can focus on delivering application functionality without the distraction of managing infrastructure. Another benefit with cloud providers is that they have startup programs where you can apply and get credits worth tens of thousands of dollars to offset your initial hosting costs.

- The specific technologies that you choose should make sense for the type of business/product you are building, the level and makeup of your team, and the support for the technical strategy you are driving. Keep in mind the principles described around proportional investment in engineering. With these initial choices you want to balance pragmatism and the need to be lean with enough of a long-term strategy not to be buried in technical debt as the business scales.

- Part of the validated learning loop is measuring experiments. Being able to define, collect, and communicate key performance metrics is important from the start. At this stage, the important metrics are around measuring the effectiveness of the MVP, product/market adoption, and customer success (things that determine if we are doing the job the customer is paying us for). Another key area (if it is important to the business) is to be able to track the ROI of the product investment and understand when things aren't working.

Things to Consider

- The definitive book on creating technical products is Marty Cagan's *INSPIRED* (2018). It is also one of the best books for understanding what a Product Manager does (or should do). It is a book that should be on every product leader's shelf.

- A great resource for the raw startup is *Running Lean* by Ash Maurya (2012). This contains the Lean Canvas and useful guides for running customer and solution discovery.

- *The Lean Startup* by Eric Ries (2011) defines the Lean Startup method and is a must-read for all product people.

- Jeff Patton's (2014) book *User Story Mapping* is the definitive source on story maps.

- *The Four Steps to the Epiphany* by Steve Blank (2013) is the book to read to understand your customer.

- As you scale your company, the following books will help you think about how to keep your culture innovative, to make sure you don't get stuck just protecting the core, and how to learn to start new things in an existing company: *Escape Velocity* by Geoffrey Moore (2011), *The Innovator's Dilemma* by Clayton Christensen (2016), and *Creativity, Inc.* by Ed Catmull (2014).

Building an Initial Data Team For Your Startup

Even though data is critical for technology companies, I've seen startups delay key activity involving data until "we reach a certain size." When they do address it, they go all-in in a big bang which can cause more problems than it fixes. A phased approach to data management is what I advocate because it will yield higher results.

Step one is to map out your data flows, where it's collected, at what frequency, in what format, and where it's consumed and surfaced. It's important to have one team, like a Data Pipeline team, be responsible for all data rather than to have each function collect their own data, otherwise you can have a mess on your hands. For example, take something as simple as counting the number of emails that have been rejected by a mailbox provider for any given customer. Suppose you want a weekly total—just sum seven days, right? But what happens if two teams choose different days of the week as the starting point? You'll end up with two parts of your product team telling your customer two different values from what should be the same data. That could easily lead to a lack of trust in the system overall and increase the churn risk.

The Data Pipeline team can create standard roll-up tables to transform the data with tags as it transitions through the pipeline. That way the Product teams can focus on delivering customer value rather than data manipulation.

Step two is to hire a data analyst, a generalist who can pull data from anything, like Google Sheets, Salesforce, Hubspot, or anywhere else. You don't need to invest in heavy BI tools at this time; instead, spend your energy (and money) on establishing more important things like a unique key that spans your data sources—CRM, Platform, and Support. That will unlock more value than fancy graphs and charts and will give you insight into the health of the business and guide investments.

Step three: consider hiring a data scientist. This person needs to be carefully managed and will typically sit on a project within engineering because they'll need access to data and a way to implement their solutions. But I've seen a tendency for data scientists to quickly build an initial model and tune it to produce "good enough" results and then watched them spend weeks and months trying to perfect it. A trap you can all too easily fall into is getting swept up in the excitement of what the data can tell you and to keep pushing for more without ever releasing the value along the way.

Finally, once you've got the output from your data scientist, you'll need to integrate it back into your mainstream engineering teams. There might be initial resistance from the engineering teams since data scientists rarely align with them, but a data engineer with roles in both data science and engineering can smooth the implementation. A good data engineer should have enough experience to highlight work with the Production Engineering teams to resolve data issues, but you need to ensure that somebody in this chain of data custody is thinking holistically.

David Wilby, *Former (at various times) Chief Product Officer, Chief Operating Officer, Chief Data Officer, Return Path*

9

Hiring Product Development Team Members

Hiring and building teams are the most important things you will do as a leader. People make an immediate impact (positively or negatively) and they make a long-term impact; again, positively or negatively. There's no better way to create the culture you want than to hire people who will help you accelerate it. On the other hand, there's no better way to ruin the culture than to hire people who are not going to help you create or promote the culture you want. I certainly don't have all of the answers and I'm still learning and experimenting with what works, but after interviewing hundreds of candidates over my career and hiring 100+ people into product development roles, I've learned a few things that I'd like to share with you.

First, you need to be clear about what you're looking for in a new hire and this involves close collaboration with your team and with other functional areas. Obviously, you won't consider hiring someone to just plug a current hole or gap; you'll want to think about how the role can grow with the company as it scales. We'll talk a bit more about this in career pathing, but you need to have a roadmap in mind for the product development organization, the individual, and the company before you even start vetting candidates.

We have broken this topic up into some chapters: interviewing (Chapter 10), onboarding (Chapter 10), increasing the funnel and building diverse teams (Chapter 11), retaining and career pathing people (Chapter 12), and growing your bench (Chapter 13).

Interviewing

Interviewing is more than asking a few standard questions or putting a candidate through a stress test to see how they respond. It's an opportunity to understand a person better and an opportunity for you to provide a clear picture for them on what your culture is, what you value, what exciting projects you have coming up, and what their future might look like if they join your team.

Interviewing involves the following, and you ought to be very prepared and organized because you're driving the process. That means asking good questions and keeping things on track even if it means stopping someone from talking with the statement, "Let's move on to X."

The Audition

With product development roles, having candidates demonstrate their skills is a core part of an interview—especially with engineering hires. How you learn about a person's skills is important though, because it defines your hiring culture and drives the type of results you get from candidates and from your hiring process. For instance, a number of technology companies have an interview process that values deep algorithmic expertise and puts candidates on the spot on a whiteboard, asking candidates to regurgitate their computer science knowledge. While that approach might be required to find the absolute smartest engineers you can find, you will also overlook other key attributes that you want in a team member. The "let's figure out how smart you are" approach attracts certain types of engineers, but excludes a bunch of others who are great problem solvers. Maybe they are more intimidated or don't think as well in high pressure environments.

At Return Path, a problem-solving audition was important but we went about trying to make it as close to a normal experience as we could so that we could assess the candidate in their natural environment. We wanted to learn how they work but more importantly, how they work with others. Are they collaborative? Do they seek advice and counsel from others? Before we brought a candidate onsite, we would give them a small project to complete to whatever level of detail they wanted. The project was intentionally vague so that we could see how creative they would be at interpreting the requirements and getting a start on the solution. And, isn't that the reality of most startups, where everyone is involved in figuring out what they are building with loose requirements? What better way to see if candidates struggle with not having detailed requirements? For us, if they had a difficult time in this situation, that's probably not a good fit anyway.

When candidates come onsite, we ask them to bring their computer and development environment with their code example. Having their own computer is a key item for creating a natural environment for an engineer. I (Shawn) always hated doing technical interviews on someone else's workstation with a development environment that I had never used; I didn't want candidates to have to do that. I want to remove the variables that are introduced from the stress of the interview and the lack of comfortable technology as much as possible. If the candidate is struggling, I want that to be a strong data point and not me guessing that maybe they just can't type because of the split keyboard we put in front of them.

Next, we have them walk through the code they wrote. This is a great icebreaker for them because they are in the driver's seat and are leading the discussion. They aren't being asked hard-ball questions right off the top or staring at a problem for the first time in front of a room full of strangers. And, there are so many data points that you get from their pre-work. How much time did they spend on the problem? Did they introduce any novel approaches to solving by writing their own algorithms or did they rely on libraries? Did they write tests? Did they comment their code? Then we give them a new dataset and ask them to run their code against our dataset instead of the 10 toy records that they got with the original assignment. Of course, our data typically breaks their code and we spend the rest of the time in a debug loop with them and a couple of engineers who are part of the team interview process. This brings in a totally different part of the process because we then get to understand how they debug and collaborate with the team around them to solve things that they haven't seen before.

The audition provides us with a really good picture of a candidate's ability to design systems, solve problems, fix bugs, talk about quality and scaling, and collaborate with others. It is a well-rounded development experience that is more like a day-in-the-life of an engineer than a few "gotcha" questions proving a person remembers their computer science theory from college. A practical audition process is one of the key reasons we hired well in engineering at Return Path. We also used a form of an audition for Product Management, UX, Data Science, and leadership roles. They were all designed around a practical problem with some work at home ahead of time and a presentation or collaborative whiteboard design session.

As we're writing this, the world is dealing with the COVID-19 pandemic, and we are thinking about how this changes things regarding interviewing and remote collaboration. The good news is that the process described for interviewing can be done remotely—as a matter of fact, we hired a number of engineers that we interviewed remotely using this same audition process. The difference is that now these engineers will be working remotely as well, so you may want to incorporate a few other practices in your interviewing process. The interview process will be fully remote and you might want to spread out the schedule to accommodate the different interviewers that will be involved—besides, everything doesn't have to be scheduled back to back since the candidate isn't coming onsite. That schedule could be better for the candidate too since it might be hard to schedule a full-day for interviews. There will also be more of a focus on how the candidate communicates and manages their schedule since they will be working more independently and will need to overcome the communication challenges of being remote.

The Practical Interview Process

Another part of our interview process, after the audition, was a series of team-based interviews that covered experience, culture, work style, and fit. We always approached this as a team, because we were such a collaborative group that we wanted to stress this during interviews and make sure that candidates were getting a full representation of what it would be like to work with our team. It also gave us the ability to mentor employees who were new to interviewing since they were encouraged to attend and listen and maybe just ask a couple of questions that they had prepared ahead of time with their manager. Having new and experienced team members participate in the interview kept the quality of the interview high and provided a better experience for the candidate. Another benefit of getting the team involved is to showcase your culture. A candidate who only interviews with a handful of employees doesn't have a full picture of what it's like to work at a company, what the company values, and how diverse and creative the teams are. It was typical for a candidate who interviewed at Return Path to talk to 15–20 people (in small groups of no more than four people) and to meet many more during their onsite visit.

Finally, the other thing to stress with interviewing is the importance of respecting people's time and being the type of company that the candidate wants to work for even if they don't get the job. We always reminded the recruiting and interviewing teams that we wanted a declined candidate's reaction to be, "That's too bad I didn't get the job—I hope I get another chance sometime and definitely want to work here in the future." That means that every candidate who applies should receive a nice personal note that the timing wasn't right and that we will consider them in the future for other roles. If a candidate doesn't make it past a phone interview or in-person interview, they should still receive a personal note or a call saying that it didn't work out but that they should try again later. Respecting a candidate's time and effort also meant that we never interrupted an interview in the middle and walked someone out (unless there was an obvious behavioral issue). We interviewed and were fully engaged with a candidate until the end because they had invested a bunch of time in preparing for the interview and it was important for us to spend time with them and provide thoughtful feedback about why it didn't work out. If we had bad candidates after the initial phone interview, it was because something broke down in an early stage and that's on us. That's something we need to fix, not something that we take out on the candidate.

Onboarding

Your job isn't done after the candidate accepts the offer, it actually continues through the first 90 days. It is critical to have a plan beyond providing them a desk, laptop, monitor, and a ton of paperwork. Creating a strong product development team culture starts with a robust onboarding process. In Product Development we didn't just rely on the HR team to do the onboarding, we had our own process that kicked off on Day 1. Some of the things that we did included a 2-hour meeting with the hiring manager going through a deck about the business and our products, introducing the new hire to the product development team and our practices, providing information on how to find things out on their own, introduction to their mentor, and taking them out for a casual team lunch. At the end of the day the new hire would write up their 30-60-90-day goals based on conversations with their manager.

As a manager, one of the best things you can do to get a new hire off on the right foot is to set expectations and the framework for communication. In my experience, most conflict is created by mismatched expectations and miscommunication, so getting this right at the start is the key to having a great team member. In communicating with a new hire, it is helpful to lead by sharing your values and leadership style—and include within that discussion your "operating manual" for how to work best with you. It is also helpful to cover the interaction points between you and them, and between them and the team they will be working with. These interaction points include one-to-ones, stand ups, time with their mentor, peer reviews, and collaboration across teams.

One of the best frameworks to set clear expectations is visual, where you draw a horizontal line on a page or whiteboard and tell the new hire that the line represents the expectations for their role, something defined that they are responsible for. Then place a dot just under the line that represents their current position (or performance) with an arrow leading up and to the right from the dot that represents their trajectory. Make it very clear that the new hire owns their current position and they "own" their effort and trajectory for their growth. Your role as CTO/CPO, your responsibilities, are to help, coach, find resources, and clear any obstacles to make them successful, but they are responsible for their success. You own the expectation line and ultimately some point in the future where we admit that it's not working. In cases of performance issues, that timeline for a decision on staying with the company or leaving is made very clear to the new hire so that they understand it. For new hires that initial timeline is 90 days and it isn't about scaring them, but providing a really clear framework with a bunch of support to help them ramp up, contribute, and be successful. Finally, it's helpful to use a detailed plan with the framework where you can collaborate on goals and outcomes that drive the specifics and create accountability for the new hire. The goals include specific tasks and learning items for each 30-day period with a key outcome or demonstrated deliverable.

Here is an example of the types of things that we included in our engineering 30-60-90-day onboarding goals:

- **First 30 days.** Complete all onboarding documents, build relationships within and outside the team, and learn and understand all systems. Work on story cards around distinct pieces of work to support learning the system and to contribute to quarterly goals. At the end of the first 30-day period, the new hire will teach back to the team the key systems and conduct a reverse interview with leadership.

- **Second 30 days**. Demonstrate that you can work independently in small distinct areas of the system. At the end of the second 30-day period the new hire will run a demonstration to the larger team of a feature/change they implemented.

- **Third 30 days.** On their own, the new hire must demonstrate that they can drive larger projects/epics independently and they need to participate in the on-call rotation. At the end of the third 30-day period the new hire will provide a tech talk or product update to the business or their peers.

Bootcamps

Another useful process to introduce to new hires are bootcamps. Bootcamps are particularly useful in engineering where you have certain central processes and practices that you want everyone to be aware of and trained on, but bootcamps are also useful across other teams too. A bootcamp is a more informal setting where you can have courses on leadership values, innovation, and agile processes that are key for product development teams to know and key for others across the company to know, too. Courses on the business domain are also really valuable to new hires (and provide updates and refreshers to others) that are taught by others with expertise. While bootcamps typically require a larger employee base or consistent hiring flow, they can be done informally (even one-to-one) and have the side-effect of making sure things are documented and consistently taught. A couple other key side effects of bootcamps are that they are really good for recurrent training across the company or for employees who want to learn about other areas of the business. Because bootcamps provide a broad view of the company, they provide a window to the new hire and others about career pathing and they expose new hires to other employees across the company who lead the training.

That expectation line that is drawn for a new hire in their first few days is more than a line and their starting point. It involves lots of deliverables by the new hire and by the product development team to ensure that the person not only has the opportunity to learn about the company, but the opportunity to interact with others so that they don't live in a bubble. One of our core values is collaboration and our onboarding process will highlight any red flags that a person is not going to fit with the team.

10

Increasing the Funnel and Building Diverse Teams

A lot of people talk about building diverse teams, a lot of people wish for that, but if you're not intentional about it, it will never happen. We were intentional at Return Path about building diverse teams. We believe that Product Development is a profoundly creative profession and that the quality of the work is lower if you lack diversity—diversity in people, in experiences, in ideas, and in approaches. Without diversity you're worse off as a product development team. Creativity depends on life experiences that we get when we broaden our stereotypes of who an engineer, product manager, or data scientist is. While building diverse teams takes longer on the whole, it returns better results in the long term. Non-diverse, homogeneous teams of like-minded people who have deep experience working together are naturally faster at collaborating and getting something going quickly, but their solutions can often be one-dimensional, and non-diverse teams lack the creativity and tenacity to think differently about problems and approach problems from a different angle. When we broadened our candidate pool, removed biases, and searched for people who didn't fit the traditional stereotype of an engineer, we generated a number of key (positive) side effects:

- We had really interesting candidates to choose from to continue to help us build even more diverse teams.

- Diversity has a positive impact. When you have diverse teams and you interact with people at career fairs and interviews, they want to learn more, especially when they see an engaged, diverse team of people who are proud to work for a company. The best way to attract diverse talent is to be diverse yourself.

- It allowed us to be competitive in areas (New York, Denver, Austin) that were difficult to hire in because we weren't just trying to go up against Google, Amazon, Facebook, and others all the time—we were looking for non-traditional candidates and had more to offer for some candidates.

To find diverse talent, you don't compromise on your hiring criteria, but open your funnel and find people who have been marginalized by the traditional tech screening process. In Chapter 9 we mentioned how we designed our audition process to be more friendly to candidates who were burnt out on the traditional interview screening process that puts them in high pressure situations where they have to regurgitate all of their computer science knowledge. That helped attract different candidates and helped them relax so that we could get the best performance out of them during the short time that we had to gauge their skills. It also helped to include a diverse mix of employees in the hiring process, including at the top of the funnel at career fairs and phone screens, as well as at in-person interviews. You gather new data points when building diverse teams. One day I (Shawn) was in an interview with a male candidate and the technical audition was being led by a strong female engineer. Every response or follow-up that the candidate gave was directed at me or the other male engineer in the room instead of to the female engineer who asked the question. I would redirect him by saying, "Don't look at me, she asked you the question," but I had seen enough to realize that this candidate would not be a strong fit with the type of culture and team we were building. I shudder to realize the hiring mistakes we would have made if we didn't have the right interview team in place to pick up on stuff like this.

Other ways to increase the top of the funnel and find overlooked candidates include building internship/genius-academy programs, using returnships, and incorporating blind auditions. Here are a few examples.

- **Paid internship.** We ran a paid internship called the Email Genius Academy at Return Path every summer and accepted 5–15 interns. The whole company participated, but the main concentration was around product development roles. We attended key career fairs every spring with a diverse group of employees who represented our culture and values and were warm and inviting—attracting similar candidates. By creating a welcoming and inclusive screening process, we were able to bring in interns each year who weren't just traditional engineering students but were problem solvers, curious about the business and eager to learn. We didn't give them "gopher" internship work either, they got a meaty business-focused project that would take up at least two months of their internship and a mid- to senior engineering partner to mentor them through it and help report back to the team and business at the end of their internship. We also accepted junior and some sophomore interns who would return to school the following year and tell their friends about the great experience they had working at Return Path, and word would spread, reinforcing our values and ensuring that we had interesting candidates seeking us out each spring.

- **Returnship.** Returnships or re-entry programs for women who have been away from the workplace is another way to find really strong candidates who have been overlooked simply because they don't have recent experience but were really strong employees earlier in their career. Return Path started a re-entry program in 2014 (that was eventually spun out to a non-profit organization called Path Forward), which was a four-month paid internship program designed for women who had been out of the workforce for more than two years to re-enter and build credible and relevant experience, and to expand the talent pool for our organization. Lisa Stephens is a great example of a talented software engineer who left IBM in 1992 to stay home and raise her children and was looking to go back to work over 20 years later. She had successfully brought her skills up to speed through coding schools, and online programs, but wasn't seeing any interest from employers. Lisa was part of the Path Forward inaugural class, and we hired her as a full-time software engineer at the end of the internship. Having a candidate who comes in with this much experience and only needs to update their skills to the latest technology is a win-win. Lisa was a strong engineer at Return Path and has gone on to be an engineering manager, expanding her impact and influence.

- **Removing bias.** Another program we used at Return Path was our partnership with GapJumpers. GapJumpers is a company working to remove workplace bias through diagnosing and improving your hiring practices. We used GapJumpers to host our audition process and do the initial screening of some of our candidates to experiment with blind auditions and to generally expand our funnel to find non-traditional candidates. This didn't work for more senior roles, since those candidates wanted to talk to a hiring manager earlier in the process instead of doing a bunch of work first without a guaranteed interview, but it worked for some of our associate and mid-level roles. Having a hiring manager review working code or a project plan before meeting a candidate or reviewing their resume flipped the whole process around and brought candidates to the forefront who would easily have been screened out by just looking at their resume. It tended to find people who had the tenacity, drive, and work ethic to stand out—people who were taking charge of their career and not just coasting on entitlement. It challenged our thinking about where problem solvers and programmers come from, and through it we hired engineers, product managers, and data scientists who were previously retail store managers, salespeople, and account managers.

11

Retaining and Career Pathing People

What about after a new hire has been with the company for 90 days? How do you retain a great hire? Well, assuming you have the right foundation in place, you're most of the way there. That means that the culture is right, the employee is on a great team, they are solving interesting problems, and they can connect the dots between the work that they do and business outcomes. But, that isn't quite enough. Having a career trajectory is important and people want to know what comes after the role that they are doing now. Early stage companies often fall into the trap of thinking that people will just be satisfied to contribute in their current role for a long time if the projects are interesting and the company is growing. We had that issue at Return Path too, initially giving everyone the title of software engineer even though it was clear that there were big differences between people's skills. Now, of course, we paid people differently based on their experience and responsibilities, but there was no published career path in Engineering that people could track against, and it started to cost us as more senior people realized that in order to move to the next level, they had to move out of the company. We learned an important lesson that even if titles weren't important to us, they were important to people who wanted to know where they were at in their career progression and the next level they could aim for as they improved their skills.

We tried over a few years to put a career development framework in place and learned as we went along. The first version only introduced two roles (software engineer and senior software engineer), had 60+ attributes, took 90 minutes for engineers to assess themselves against, and unintentionally created a game where engineers would try to improve a few attributes to get to the next level instead of looking at it holistically. A second version simplified it, tied it to additional roles, and involved the manager more. Finally, we created a third version that really simplified it to five core attributes consistent across levels, tied it to our core values, and incorporated team feedback and development planning. We also rolled out versions of this across Product Management, UX, and Data Science.

What we ended up with in Engineering answered the question, "Where do I stand with regard to my professional growth as an engineer, and what do I need to do to develop my career?" We framed it as only one part of your career progression to another role. It reflected your skill proficiency in your current role and your development in the next role. It was to be used as a holistic set of expectations to be successful in that role and give you aims on your development areas, not as a game to be "won." The percentages that were tracked in the framework were there to be a rough measure of proficiency in those expectations and should be set and aligned with conversations between employees and their manager. We wanted to see above 90% proficiency in their current role and at least 50% proficiency in the next role before considering employees for promotion. This ensured that people had enough skill in the next role to be successful and supported the "working out of title" to prove interest and initial skill at the next level. But that wasn't all. Just "hitting the numbers" on the career development framework didn't mean that you were automatically going to move to the next level. It was fine for engineers to remain in their current level at full proficiency and as a high performer. A promotion should happen when we have a good overlap of interest, opportunity, and qualification. Other factors that were required for a promotion were:

Engineers should be high performers to be considered for promotion to the next level.

- Promotions were reviewed every 6–12 months and reflected sustained performance over that period.

- There needed to be a business need for additional senior level roles.

- Years of professional experience don't have to line up exactly, but provide some pacing for career progression, and experience is a factor.

- Engineers eligible for promotion were reviewed by a group of their peers and engineering leadership before receiving a promotion.

The last point was key to getting everyone involved in making sure that there were going to be no surprises on promotions and was important as we got larger as an engineering organization. The biggest challenge was in having a manager who "graded easier" than another manager in another part of the company, and we made some missteps early on where we promoted someone and had a big backlash across engineering because that individual was good at managing up to their manager but didn't have credibility across their peers. Having a group of peers and alignment across engineering leadership were key in making sure that promotions made sense and had alignment.

We ended up with the following roles and responsibilities in Engineering:

- Associate Software Engineer: entry-level role, curious, learning quickly, solves scoped problems, and contributes to the team.

- Software Engineer: significant contributor, owns projects from beginning to end, collaborates, gives feedback, incremental, and proportional.

- Senior Software Engineer: recognized leader and key decision-maker on the team, solid stakeholder manager, collaborates between teams, and takes a rigorous engineering approach.

- Principal Software Engineer: recognized leader in engineering, responsible for core systems and projects, collaborates across engineering, and carries the engineering brand within the company.

12

Hiring and Growing Leaders

Next to hiring well, the next important thing is to make sure you have the right leaders in place and that you are continuing to develop the bench of future leaders. Hiring leaders externally is difficult to get right. You are looking for people who are highly aligned with the culture and practices that you are building and who have the ability to build trust and rapport on the teams they will be responsible for. They also need to be a good leader, with both the skills to work effectively with people and the ability to get the team to execute and hit business outcomes. Finally, especially with technical roles, the leader needs to have deep experience as a contributor in the area that they will be managing. When you take all of this together, you can see how challenging it can be to find the right person who covers all of these areas. Typically, it is easier to hire a leader into an organization that already has a strong leadership team—that peer team provides a center of gravity for the new leader and a chance for the new leader to pair with an established leader on a team for a period before taking over. Even then you can have mixed results with hiring leaders externally. The biggest misses have been getting people who weren't fully aligned with the culture we were building and creating pockets in engineering with different values or approaches to engineering. Or, we'd get people who were strong technically but weren't strong people managers and lacked the empathy to build a deep connection with the people they were leading. Or, we would get people who were only strong people managers and lacked the technical experience to build respect with the team. You get the point. It's not easy to fill senior technical leadership roles!

One option that works well is to find a strong individual contributor who is trying to take a leadership track in their career and is blocked at their current company either because leadership there doesn't feel they are ready yet or because there just isn't an open opportunity right now. You can hire them and have them join a team as an individual contributor for a few months to learn the systems and build trust with the team. When (and if) the timing is right, you can then move them into a leadership role on that team—it could be a tech lead initially and then to a full front-line manager role.

By far, the best approach is developing leaders internally. Again, it starts with hiring—looking for those extra leadership qualities beyond someone's experience and skill to just do the individual contributor job. It is about looking for the engineer who loves to solve business problems, not just technical ones, or the product manager who wants to start their own business someday. It's about finding a UX engineer who is completely passionate about product design and can't stop asking questions about your customers or the data scientist who is all about data-driven decision making. It's about looking for candidates who can do the job and are especially empathetic, connect well with people, and who are wired to lead. This doesn't have to be true for every hire, but if you start to look for these additional qualities, you will begin to build a bench of talented leaders with high potential to be future leaders as you help them develop.

And speaking of helping them develop, you need to provide multiple opportunities for individual contributors to take on ownership and leadership roles to give them experience and opportunities to work "out of title." At Return Path, we developed leaders through leadership development bootcamps, through mentoring relationships, through technical leadership opportunities on teams and certain technologies, and through opportunities to lead and present during hackathons, engineering summits, tech talks, and lunch and learns.

When we had an opportunity to put a front-line manager in place and we had a good internal candidate, we followed the 30-60-90-day plan that was part onboarding and part testing that this was a good fit. Our approach ultimately became a framework to turn individual contributors into managers. This is what that plan looked like—with credit to David Loftesness, Twitter's former Director of Engineering and the original inspiration for this:

Day 0. Discussion to make sure you know what you are getting into as a first-time manager. These are the truths about the job that you have to accept and the adjustments that you have to make—coding less, having a calendar full of meetings, leading by enabling others to do the work, setting the ends and letting the team figure out the means. We also want to make sure motivations are right: Don't become a manager in order to just please the boss; don't become a manager only to advance your career; do become a manager if growth for you involves others; do become a manager if you channel empathy; do become a manager if you can give the trust you ask of others.

First 30 days. Block off time to learn. This includes a reading list and our Engineering Leadership Playbook; it includes joining the bi-weekly engineering leadership peer support meeting; it includes working with your manager and mentor to shadow them as they manage the team—including joining them on one-to-ones. At this point you are still taking 60% of individual contributor work.

Second 30 days. Balancing between individual contributor and manager. Take on one-to-ones by yourself; lead more of the team ceremonies (planning, standups, etc.); balance your current development work, including ramping down the number of cards you were picking up as an individual contributor to about 30% or so.

Third 30 days. Ramping up to be the full-time manager. In the final 30 days, you have ramped down your individual contributor work and are taking on all of the management responsibilities for the team.

During these 90 days we let new managers slowly take on more responsibility for the team, but as a practice didn't make them have performance conversations, write reviews, or handle compensation matters. Along the way we tell the new manager that three things have to line up at the end before we finalize the role. That is: (1) the CTO/CPO has to like how it's working; (2) the team has to like it; and (3) most importantly, you have to like how it's working. As the leader who is developing this new manager, try to spend time mentoring and meeting with the team to gauge the impact that the new manager is having and getting to this decision point on day 90. We've done this process with over a dozen new leaders and only had one person elect to go back to being an individual contributor at the end—and in that situation the process worked and saved the team from having a leader who wasn't passionate about being in that position. And actually, the feedback we received from that individual was that they were overwhelmed with how much the team vented and they were unsure that they wanted to deal with all of the needs the team had. Without that person doing actual one-to-ones, they never would have figured this out along the way before becoming the full-time manager. As you scale your organization, the temptation will be to quickly promote people into front-line managers to handle the growth. Our cautionary advice is to take your time and pay attention to the process and wait until the manager candidate is really ready. It's far better to overload a good manager temporarily with too many direct reports than putting a mediocre manager in place or prematurely promoting a new manager. You have to get this right as you grow—the number one reason people leave companies is still because of their manager.

Developing leaders internally this way has been the most successful model and leaders promoted into first-line managers have gone on to become Senior Managers, Directors, and VPs.

Other Things to Consider

While "smart" and "get things done" are two key characteristics to look for while hiring, there are a couple other things to look for, and here are a few questions we would use to determine if those attributes are lacking:

- You can typically figure out how senior or experienced someone is by having them articulate what they hate about a process or company practice or programming language. If they are just getting started (or started a long time ago but haven't really grown up), little things will bother them, things that they could fix if they were more experienced or mature. The more experienced a person is, the more likely that what they "hated" was a big problem, something that shows that they really dug deep and addressed some hard problems.

- Ask individual contributors about someone's career they improved to test how empathetic and collaborative they are. This is also a good proxy to determine their potential to move into a leadership role.

- The more details someone remembers about past projects they worked on, the better they are at caring about details and the better they are at getting things done. It's always a surprise when someone is asked to talk about the hardest problem they solved or to talk about the details of a recent project and how they went about it, and they can't quite remember or articulate the key parts of the project.

- Ask engineers about the last piece of code they wrote to see how they think about decomposing problems and how they structure their code. It is also one of those questions that either gets immediate engagement or a quizzical look that reveals their passion (or lack of it).

- Look for someone (or encourage them) to teach you something. Often, the best hires are ones you learn something from during the interview process that makes you want to work with them. It doesn't just have to be in their area of technical expertise, but in any area.

People are the core of your business and hiring is the most important decision you will make. A post on Quora years ago by Michael O. Church where he answered a question about firing an employee with this simple and brilliant summary about the types of people in an organization is spot-on:

The best employees are multipliers who make others more productive, and next are the adders (workhorses). Subtracters are the good-faith incompetents who cost more than they bring. Dividers are the worst kind of problem employee: they bring the whole team (or company) down.

We think of this quote and refer to it as the "Math Model to People Management." The goal is to hire, retain, and develop people to be multipliers and adders. Subtractors are developing contributors who cost more than they produce—and all new hires start as subtractors. As outlined in the Onboarding section in Chapter 10, your goal as a leader is to turn them into adders and multipliers or be specific about how long they have until it isn't working. Dividers damage morale and bring the whole team down—fire them immediately.

13

Organizing, Collaborating with, and Motivating Effective Teams

If you are trying to build a development organization where people are engaged and solving business problems along with engineering problems, you need to get a few things right.

First, you'll need to create a culture of ownership that is accountability-driven. This is deeper than just defining responsibilities for people. While responsibility and accountability seem similar (and are often used interchangeably), there is a fundamental difference between the two. While people can have responsibilities, accountability is something that you take—something you do to yourself rather than something done to you. Organizations sometimes try to fix things by redefining responsibilities, but that doesn't change the way people think like personal accountability or ownership does. Ask yourself, "Is more responsibility going to lead to success here?" Accountability is empowering and whenever people get personally involved, it produces better results. This is why Agile ceremonies like Fist-to-Five (if taken seriously) are key because when team members are personally committing to the team to deliver the goals, you get better results. For leaders, this requires transparency, clear communication, direction, and getting out of the way. It means that you centralize vision and decentralize control.

Second, to build a great team, you'll need people who are curious, self-starters, and intrinsically motivated. The good news is that if you create the culture described above, you have the right foundation to attract and retain people with these qualities. People who are account-ability-driven like to work at companies that give them ownership and freedom. The key differentiator between the good and bad hires centers on the extent to which people want to hold themselves accountable.

Third, are people valued or valuable? It's pretty much table stakes now that companies "value" their employees and have cultures and perks that make people feel valued working there. The higher bar is whether or not a person understands their value to the company. In other words, can a person draw a direct line between the work they do and a company outcome? This is harder for a company to define for every person, but a deeper way to get people engaged and taking ownership is when they can connect the dots between their work and the company's success.

So, assuming that you have the foundation right, you have a team with intrinsically motivated people who take ownership, where leaders are setting outcomes and giving people the freedom to control the methods to accomplish those outcomes, then what? Your job as the product development leader is to understand how teams of people interact. The same principles apply for teams as for individuals. Teams need a vision and an outcome they can hit; they need to be motivated and have control over the methods they use to hit that outcome; they need ownership and accountability for the successes and failures of a product; and they need to have some roles and responsibilities that govern interactions with the business and other teams that they are collaborating with.

It's easier to keep teams all rowing in the same direction when the company is small with a single product that all the teams are collaborating on. It becomes increasingly difficult as the company grows and gets into additional product lines and business units. The effectiveness of each individual team taking ownership and having all of this control is now starting to backfire because the individual team outcomes or motivation are in conflict with those of another team. This is where understanding and designing the operating system at the team, department, or business unit are key to keeping a culture of ownership and accountability and pushing control to the edges while still collaborating effectively.

Next are three different examples that illustrate how to align teams so that they focus on outcomes, not output. In one example we drove higher software quality by disbanding the quality assurance team; in another example we created a unified product development organization rather than separate product and engineering organizations; and in the third example we had to manage the impedance mismatch between product and go-to-market.

Example 1: Quality

Ensuring quality is a key requirement of an effective product development team and there are many ways to do that. One common approach is to have a dedicated quality assurance (QA) team (depending on the type and stage of a company), but it comes with a cost. A QA team needs another team to coordinate with to make sure that the QA team's motivations, values, and operating system are aligned with the company's and also make sure it is working effectively with the rest of the product development organization. When it's not working well, it can slow things down, create issues between teams, and actually reduce the overall system quality that the team was created to ensure in the first place.

We had this experience while working with a dedicated QA team in a rapidly scaling, early-stage startup. We were just getting to that point of scaling out teams to handle specific products and had a shared service team that was responsible for manual and automated testing before code was released. The team was working well when the company was smaller, had less product contexts, and had a predictable release cadence. There were two key KPIs that we noticed changing that pointed to the ineffectiveness of the QA team. One was that they were becoming the bottleneck in the development sprint cycle. The second issue was a spike in production support work, which was the work that teams did to fix bugs or other issues after code was released. When we dug into the data, we noticed three core issues on the QA team that were causing this slip in performance:

1. **Context switches.** Our high growth coupled with a trend to push more decision making onto the teams created deeper technical and product contexts that the central service wasn't equipped to keep up with. The side effect was that the development engineers were having to come over and help QA engineers test the code they had just written.

2. **Lack of staffing and capability revealed we were doing one-off testing processes rather than building a suite of automation that could be generalized for all teams.** The QA team didn't have the expertise and influence to drive a standard here since most of the deep senior engineers were on the product teams and just went around them. The side-effect was that we had more conflict between teams. Teams would either go around QA, or QA would push to centralize a way of doing things to remain relevant even if it wasn't in the best interest of the business.

3. **Disconnected team members and a focus on output instead of outcomes.** The culture we created wasn't a good one because development engineers didn't have to care about being thorough and caring about quality since it was the dedicated QA team's job. The fact that QA felt disconnected from the business problem and was just focused on the output of their work was suboptimal. And the fact that QA was more concerned about looking relevant

than being able to move the business KPIs and outcome forward hurt the business.

While there are ways to fix this to keep a central team functioning well and aligned with the other teams, we decided to dismantle the dedicated QA team. This wasn't easy and it required a lot of effort framing a new philosophy around quality, how we would approach quality as a company, and then executing the change well. Not getting the framing right will work against any change you make and although we tried our best to frame our new quality approach, we still got accused years later of "not caring about quality ever since we shut down QA." We cared a lot about quality! We fixed an issue that was causing a spike in production support, but we were still misunderstood.

We ended up moving all of the QA engineers and embedding them in the product teams, and we pushed the product teams to incorporate quality into their team's process. The message was that every engineer was a QA engineer. They could build unit tests or full integration tests or incorporate more rigorous peer code reviews, but they had to come up with a process that fit their size and scale and was proportional to the business. Some teams were working on early-stage prototypes and could cut corners on quality and come back later to fill that in. Other teams were managing mission-critical systems and needed a higher level of quality. One side-effect of dismantling the QA team and embedding quality into the product teams was that teams got creative and incorporated various testing into their development flow (peer code reviews). We learned that if you give an engineer a solution, they will complain about it, but if you give them a problem, they will solve it. The other side-effect is that we had more teams building testing automation so that they didn't have to test things manually like they were before. So, we improved our quality and we got our teams to be more innovative—we improved effectiveness with a proportional investment in quality that fit what the business needed at that stage.

Example 2: Unified Product Development Organization

One of the keys to a growing, dynamic, creative business is harnessing and managing the natural conflict and tension that exist between the functional areas inside the business. Sales is pushing for something more to sell; Marketing has an event schedule planned out months in advance and wants features launched at specific dates; Customer Service wants more functionality in the product and higher quality; Product wants time to deeply solve a customer problem; Engineering wants time to make a system more efficient; and Finance wants it done on budget. Does this sound like every company you've ever worked with? This natural push and pull between functional areas in an organization creates resistance and friction that, if harnessed, makes an organization stronger and causes the leaders to learn how to challenge and compromise to get the best out of each other and get the best for the business. On the negative side, if you don't harness the friction, it can cause a business to take the path of least resistance and not challenge each other to become great. Obviously, at its worst, friction and discord can devolve into unhealthy conflict and turf wars between functional areas. If you are unsure of which type of friction you have in your organization, look for finger pointing and the equivalent of "your side of the boat is sinking" comments.

Nowhere is your approach to friction more important to get right than in the product development organization. The product development team has to navigate all of the conflicting goals between the various functions, collaborate well, make tradeoffs, and bring a great product to market. They also have to manage the natural internal conflicts and tradeoffs between engineering and product management, like roadmap prioritization, technical debt, team organization, and the balance between innovation and maintenance. Some amount of friction and healthy conflict within the product development organization can be good and can drive more engagement and better results, but if this devolves into stalemates where leaders only care about their functional areas, it can really slow things down and become toxic.

At Return Path, scaling rapidly created some dysfunction across Product Development, but it was more about teams optimizing around the path of least resistance than outright turf wars between functional areas. Fighting and disengaging—though they are opposite reactions—can have the same effect on a product development organization, making it less effective at collaborating, and at navigating the hard tradeoffs that need to happen to create great products.

There were two symptoms that stood out and pointed to a larger issue here:

1. We had strong product managers (some of whom were fairly technical) paired with engineering managers who were oriented toward being in service to the business. The engineering managers didn't always consider, or speak up about, the long-term technical implications of decisions. As we scaled, we didn't push hard enough on the full cost of technology on the business and what we needed to manage was both the current cost of products as well as the cost of building new ones. That was a bad combination and led project managers to really drive the product and technical roadmaps and optimize around what they needed to get product out the door without a strong engineering partner to navigate the technical implications of these decisions.

2. Another symptom that emerged was that teams became more output-driven than outcome-driven. If you looked at the goals for various teams, they were capturing the work that they were going to do for the quarter—and often hitting it—but, they weren't always able to tie their work to a business outcome and drive their goals around that.

Symptoms like these can sometimes reveal an inexperienced or immature leadership issue. But sometimes it is just that roles aren't defined well and there is confusion and overlap that create tension that can either be fought and defended or leaders will pull back and let another leader or team take the lead. For Return Path, it was the latter. There wasn't crisp role definition and it caused Product Management to take too much authority in some areas (especially around technical choices) and let Engineering off the hook for areas they were responsible for but not being accountable for.

A RACI model (responsible-accountable-consulted-informed) is a good tool to use to identify roles and responsibilities and to help you manage teams with high collaboration requirements. We've used that at Return Path before with good success. Another model we introduced that was simpler to communicate across teams was the "What and the Why" and the "How and the Who." Product Management owned the "What" and the "Why" and Engineering owned the "How" and the "Who."

How does this work in practice? Well, for Product Management, the "What" was obvious (our products) and they were already owning that. They were responsible for questions like: What are we going to build next? What is the priority of this? What story cards are in this next release? And what the heck do we do now? The "Why" was also obvious—to the Product Management team—but it wasn't expressed or articulated concretely so that it was difficult for the team to set goals, drive motivation, and just connect the dots between the work the team was responsible for and the business outcomes. A simple explanation to the team of "why" something is important and "why" the business cares about it goes really far in unifying a team and getting them to own that we are all in this together. The product management group knew why they were doing something, but ensuring they were accountable to articulate the "why" to the rest of the product development organization was really useful.

On the engineering side, the "Who" was obvious, too. Engineering leaders owned hiring, onboarding, and creating teams of engineers to work on products. Engineering was definitely on top of building teams and tuning them to make sure they were high functioning teams. What was more surprising to engineering leadership—and especially surprising to Product Management—was that Engineering also owned the

"How." Now obviously, Engineering always decided how they were going to architect and code something, but the "how" Engineering was dealing with was bigger. Engineering was accountable for how technology was going to be used to solve business problems; they were accountable for how technical debt was going to be managed; accountable for how tradeoffs were going to be made between the technical and product roadmaps; and accountable for how (and when) time was going to be spent on technical innovation to take on a new market.

Product managers were owning the tactical "how" and feathering work into the roadmap that engineers said they needed to deliver a feature, but there was a gap in the larger technical strategy that required time and a business case to be made. The technical strategy needed to understand and account for the collaboration and tradeoffs between product and engineering leadership that were beyond just sprint or quarterly planning. Acknowledging this larger "HOW" and getting Engineering to own it were the start to help us drive a more dynamic and creative product development organization. And, not having this role definition and accountability in place earlier was part of the reason for getting into the hole that Return Path was in. It caused us to have high technical debt.

By having ownership of the "how" and "what" together, Product and Engineering can manage and agree on "when" things get done. This is generally dictated by priority and deadlines on the Product side and scope and headcount on the Engineering side. But this is where healthy conflict and discussion between Product and Engineering really drove the most efficient outcomes for us.

Example 3: Impedance Mismatch

The third example of how to build greater collaboration stems from understanding an "impedance mismatch." An impedance mismatch is an electrical engineering term to describe when inputs and outputs of an electrical load don't match and cause signal reflection or an inefficient power transfer. That phrase is often used in technology to describe problems that occur due to differences between systems, the most popular example being the object-relational impedance mismatch. That mismatch describes issues between the database model and the programming language model. In short, it's a mismatch between what you have and what you want. An impedance mismatch describes the interface between Product Development and Go-to-Market (GTM) organizations at Return Path.

We had just started to get the product development organization firing on all cylinders again. There was good alignment and collaboration between teams, our leaders had good role definition, and were accountable for the what and the why and the how and the who. We were starting to innovate again, and we were making big changes to products that had been in market for a dozen years. But then the problems just started to move downstream. In some ways, you could say that because the business had been making small incremental changes in product over the last few years. The adjustment to innovating again and delivering large cross-company launches was surprising and stressful to the system. Sales and Service needed training, Support needed administration tools, Marketing needed predictable launch dates to schedule events around, and Finance still wanted to know how long it was going to take and how much it was going to cost. The main challenge was around coordinating the project work across all of the functional areas in the company, and what I noticed was that Go-to-Market operated more around a waterfall project planning model while our product development model was Agile. This was our impedance mismatch.

Although the mismatch was between waterfall and Agile methodologies, both models have a place in most businesses. First of all, waterfall isn't always bad even though it is often seen as a negative from the product development side of a business. It is a valid project planning framework, and you almost have to use something like this when you are doing any type of event or conference planning and have hard dates. It isn't a negative thing that sales planning, training, and marketing events were planned out a year in advance with a tight schedule. That's just the way an enterprise business needed to operate. Second, while Agile processes are optimized for adaptability and delivering small chunks of functionality continuously, Agile is also good for maintaining a constant pace and being predictable. We've had to remind many development teams that you can commit to a launch date and still be Agile. Again, it's all about tradeoffs.

So how do you reconcile waterfall and Agile? The framework that was most useful to our GTM and product development organizations was "fixed scope" vs. "fixed date." If we are going to commit to a hard launch date, then the scope of work might change to hit the date. That flexibility allowed the GTM teams to set a sales plan and a theme and date for their events. The development teams could then commit to the roadmap and get as many of the key features in as possible while still hitting the date. So the product development teams had flexibility to incorporate discovery and manage unknowns along the way. On the other hand, if it was important to launch with specific functionality, the GTM teams had to relax the date and work around a rough month or quarter timeframe and the development teams would agree to a set scope of functionality to deliver. Working through this framework had big impacts on the expectations of both groups and helped manage the impedance mismatch.

Another challenge with complex product launches across a large company is that you don't just have to make sure that you have horizontal alignment across functional areas. You also have to have vertical alignment between the individuals doing the work and their senior leaders. Coming from the product development function, we had processes to make sure that individual teams rolled up to senior leaders who were involved in setting goals, tracking progress, and giving feedback. Expectations were set and aligned, and communication was frequent and bi-directional. But what we learned was that the product development organization already worked in verticals; it was our normal practice. Pushing code, maintaining products, delivering functionality were what we did, just like breathing. Other organizations, not so much.

Our initial solution was to have a couple of salespeople attend a weekly launch meeting to help plan and coordinate their needs for launch because that would be an effective way to get stakeholders involved to make sure we weren't missing anything. And that's what we did—individual contributors from every function that was impacted by a company-wide product launch were involved. The thing we missed is that those departments aren't optimized around managing launches (like Product Development is) and they don't have a process for managing requirements and making tradeoffs and communicating with senior leaders about this work. What happened is that while product development contributors and leadership were aligned on the launch, other functional areas were not and the senior leaders in those areas were surprised and out of the loop. This caused a number of launches where things didn't go well: Support and Service weren't trained to handle inbound tickets, Sales wasn't fully trained on the functionality in the product, and Marketing didn't have collateral on the website. Obviously, this was not ideal and we needed to address the root cause and resolve it.

Our second attempt at solving the problem led us to create an executive level Product Council that met every week. It was driven by the product development executives and attended by other functional executives who were involved in company-wide launches. We also had key individual contributors who were involved in driving that specific launch also attend. The goals of the Product Council meeting were to get alignment and to over-communicate details around the launch. Part of the meeting was strategic and included talking through the roadmap, addressing the next scheduled launch, discussing tradeoffs and generating alignment across the functional areas. But part of the meeting was digging into the details for communication plans and training materials, reviewing support tickets, and doing product demos. We wanted to make sure that this group lived and breathed our roadmap, products, and launch process. In turn, we wanted them to communicate with their peers on the executive team and through their teams. Getting alignment at the top and getting vertical involvement with the individuals and teams responsible for execution were key. This Product Council didn't replace our annual or quarterly planning meetings, but it augmented them because the need for over-communication and high coordination and change happens in between the planning sessions. And launches across enterprise products in a large/complex business are hard and require a lot of planning and communication.

Things to Consider

- When you have a healthy team, it makes your job easier as a manager. It is much easier to identify performance and fit issues with an individual in the context of a team. It is much easier to challenge someone to step up because the team is counting on them. It is much easier for individuals to understand their roles and responsibilities in relation to their peers than trying to understand their manager's development plan. Individuals tend to work harder in order not to let their peers down rather than letting down their boss. Integrating a team and collaborating fit our management style at Return Path since we believe that if we have to manage a person extrinsically, then we've failed. We're not going to tell a person what time to come to work or tell them they can't take vacation time, but we can tell them to coordinate with the team and don't let the team down.

- In 2015, a group in Google's People Operations released some research answering the question "What makes a Google team effective?" They found a few key dynamics like dependability, clear goals, and impact, but far and away the most important factor was psychological safety. It makes sense—if team members don't feel safe around each other to admit mistakes, ask the dumb question, or try something crazy and fail, then it limits the potential of the team. On the flip side, a team with high psychological safety is more likely to engage in taking risks, experimenting, harnessing creative ideas, and being effective collaborators. Getting the culture right and building effective teams (across the whole company) is foundational to success.

- Large cross-functional planning sessions can be really good to get stakeholders from across the company to collaborate together, build empathy for each other's departments, and make important tradeoffs that build ownership. We did a quarterly Agile Roadmapping exercise and used a massive whiteboard where each team laid out their own roadmaps in horizontal swim lanes. Once all of the teams were done, they linked cards together with string to represent interdependencies. This model quickly identified bottlenecks and helped prioritize work items that multiple teams were dependent on early in the planning cycle.

14

Due Diligence and Lessons Learned from a Sale Process

As the company grows, you will have opportunities to accelerate growth or fill a hole by acquiring another company. At Return Path, we ran technical diligence on over 10 companies—acquiring five of them. Here are some of the things that a Product or Engineering leader needs to know about doing buy-side diligence.

First, you have to understand the purpose of the acquisition. Are we doing this to fill a hole in our product offering, do we need this technology, or are we really interested in the team as more of an acqui-hire? Next, you should evaluate if buying this company is the only or best way to get this product, technology, or team. Can we grow the team a bit and build it ourselves? Can we partner with a company or license the technology? Really think through the long-term implications of acquiring a company. Sometimes the opportunity and acquisition come together so easily that it distracts you from the deeper issues of integration—and that's where the real challenges are.

The product could look great on the surface but be hard to use or hard to sell; the business could have legal, financial, or data privacy risk deep in the past that you aren't aware of; the technology could be a pile of shortcuts held together by a hero engineer who isn't planning to stay after the acquisition; the team may look like a culture fit on the surface, but the people are used to operating differently and aren't going to make it through the integration. Make sure to walk through these scenarios and talk to peers who have experience with successful and failed acquisitions before you proceed. Finally, if you choose to acquire, make sure that you have a rigorous diligence process that uncovers as many of the risks as possible and provides the data you need to evaluate the tradeoffs between building versus buying.

When running a diligence process on a potential acquisition target, you typically have a small team covering the key areas of Finance, Operations, Legal, and Product/Technology. For larger acquisitions with many employees, we would include the People team. One practice is to evaluate privacy and security during the technology diligence, but often bring dedicated team members in for larger or more complicated acquisitions. Here are the key areas t in product and technology diligence and some of the details to look for:

People

Always start with people in a diligence process. As mentioned before, people are the key to any company and by talking with them first, you remove the potential awkwardness of a diligence process and you learn so much about the business. Start with one-to-ones with each team member in Product Development and ask about their background, strengths and development areas, experience with the company, and concerns that they have about being acquired. Spend time selling them on your company, how past acquisitions have gone, and what the integration process looks like. These initial conversations help each person learn about each other and build trust so they know what to expect and that helps them feel comfortable opening up and sharing more about the business. The main things to look for in these conversations is to understand the strength of each team member, if any of them are critical path, a sense of the quality of the team and culture, and—most importantly—any challenges, concerns, and operational or technical deficiencies that provide a roadmap for how to navigate the rest of the diligence.

Team

It's important to understand the culture and health of the team—their team operating systems, communication styles, decision-making process, any conflict, the way they manage ownership and accountability, and their relationship with failure. Most of the qualitative details are discovered in my one-to-ones with individuals, and the rest through conversations with product managers and the leadership team. Look for quantitative details by having someone walk through recent project and Agile team stats and look for healthy velocity and a breakdown of the type of work the team is spending time on (feature, production support, technical debt, etc.). Another key area to dig in is around overall resource allocation and how teams are staffed and how planning is done. Ask the leadership team what is missing and how they would use more money or people if they had them. There are often a number of key things that emerge when you understand the corners that are being cut by an understaffed team.

Product

The key thing to look for on the product side is efficacy—how well does the product work? How well does it solve the problem? And do customers love it? Start with having someone do a product demo and walk through the core functionality. What is the origin story of the product—how was it started? When did it get to product/market fit? How has it evolved? Who are the key customers? How do they use it? Is the product a "vitamin" or a "pain killer"? What does the near and long-term roadmap look like? If it is an early-stage company, pay attention to the discovery process, how well they have achieved product/market fit, and talk to their customers. Make sure you understand if the company has traction or just looks like it does. For later-stage companies, you should be able to look at product and financial metrics to see evidence of a strong product/market fit and a healthy growth trajectory.

System Overview

The key thing to look for on the technical side is efficiency—how well is it designed? Where is the technical debt? How does it scale from a cost and capacity standpoint? Have the technical team walk through the technical systems and outline the core functionality and how each service works in the whole. For each service, understand the key metrics (throughput and latency), look for any recent production support issues (and any recurring issues), and determine the capacity plan for scaling, the overall complexity of that service and the effort to operate it, and what the technical roadmap looks like. Holistically, you want to look for how well everything works together, what shortcuts were taken and how much technical debt exists, how complex the code base is and if the team generally is focused on outcomes or only on solving technical problems.

Privacy/Security

A lot of this is uncovered during the system overview, but it warrants a separate discussion because it is really critical and highlights areas of potential risk. You also learn a lot by a team's attitude and transparency around talking about these issues. On the security side, it is important to uncover any past security breaches, security processes in place, penetration test results, any audit controls and results, and the general process that is used to ensure security is built into the design and development process. On the privacy side, look at what data is stored and transmitted, the systems involved, and encryption controls that are in place. Work with your legal team to review the privacy policy and alignment of the company's data behaviors to that policy. With larger or international companies, it is helpful to work with outside counsel on complex deals to ensure that there are no hidden data privacy risks related to mistakes the company may have made around consent and use of data in the product.

IP and Legal Risks

Similar to security and privacy, a number of risks exist around intellectual property and software licenses. Again, you will be partnering with your internal legal team on this, but you will want to verify some key items. Make sure that you get a list of all of the employees and contractors that have been involved in building the product and make sure that those contracts cover a release for work product and, if not, make sure you can secure a release from those individuals before you inherit this liability. Ensure you look at all commercial and open source software licenses in use by the product to make sure that everything is in good standing. There could be hidden costs to operating systems when you find out that they are using a community edition service from when they were pre-revenue that now requires a large licensing fee. For large and complex acquisitions, you can pay external companies to scan code bases to find license violations or whole blocks of code copied from a licensed product and being used unlicensed. This area is critical for really understanding what you have and making sure that you don't have a ticking time bomb legal issue that an external party will bring up after the acquisition, creating unexpected costs and legal issues.

Costs

Most of this comes up in the system overview as well, but it is important to get a clear picture of the ongoing fixed and variable costs to operating the systems. The headcount costs will most likely be modeled by your team members responsible for the financial and operational parts of diligence. You should still collect and evaluate employee comp and titles and how it fits within your organization for integration down the road. On the system side, try to get a detailed breakdown of the costs per service. Pay attention to the variable and unit costs incurred for scaling and make sure that you are comfortable with the cost curve and any one-time technical costs required to scale.

Risk Assessment

The last step is to do the analysis, risk assessment, and recommendation. This includes the financial model—assuming additional investment to fill in the gaps on the team and scaling systems—to justify the acquisition and show the payback and return on the investment. You'll likely be doing this in collaboration with the financial diligence lead. You need to compare and contrast this acquisition against other options like building it yourself, licensing a solution, or partnering with another company. When doing the buy/build analysis, make sure to consider key tradeoffs like opportunity cost, technical skill required, operational requirements, and whether technology for this area needs to be a competitive strategy or more of a utility. Make sure you detail the risks in rank order including integration risks around culture and people. You will be collaborating with the rest of your diligence team and the business on this analysis, making sure to understand the impact this decision has on various stakeholders, and being able to present a business case with the trade-offs. Finally, make a recommendation backed up by your evaluation and results of your diligence.

Having done a few acquisitions, we can say that it doesn't always go well and we regret at least two of the five companies that we've been part of acquiring over the last 10 years. Here are some lessons learned and things to watch out for:

- It's not over until everyone has signed. A smart acquisition target is pursuing multiple offers and negotiating to get the best value. Be detailed around Letters of Intent and no-shop agreements and make sure you are paying attention to the timing and boundaries of these agreements during diligence. We've seen a company walk away at the last minute—legally—to pursue a better offer because we weren't on top of things.

- Make sure you know where the technical bodies are buried. Reviewing and understanding critical services and their scaling characteristics are important. Don't just take the technical co-founder's word for it. We experienced an order of magnitude volume of growth on a service after acquiring it that had an exponential cost curve to operate. It took us months to find the time to properly refactor it to get to a cost curve that we were happy with and had to eat the cost in the meantime. A deeper understanding of the system and capacity plan would have identified this during diligence.

- Don't buy the technology without the team. Unless it is just a competitive takeout acquisition or they use the exact same stack as your engineering team, you are going to have a challenge integrating and operating a company's systems without any of their technical team. Don't ask us how we know this.

- Really understand if they actually have product/market fit or it just looks like it. With early-stage acquisitions, it is important to really get into the product discovery details and talk to customers. Some founders are really good at selling up (kind of like managing up) and have a really good story about their solution and how much customers love it. I've seen startups with special pricing for beta/charter customers or continuing to keep customers connected after they've churned. Make sure you deeply understand how valuable the solution is to customers and how much they are really paying for the solution.

15

Selling Your Company

Preparation

At some point in a company's journey there will be an opportunity to sell the company or raise another round and you will be pulled in to sell-side diligence. The time to prepare for that is months or years before, not when it happens.

Now, of course, companies get opportunistic offers before they are ready to sell and get the process done without preparing well in advance, but from my experience, there are certain areas that you want to track from the beginning that make a sale process go easier. And, since the goal of most businesses is to grow and eventually sell, why not invest in this work upfront? So, one key for a successful sale is preparation. The other key is being able to tell a good story about the stage the business is at and the processes that are in place that make sense for that stage. Let's dig into both of these. Chapter 16 covers telling the story.

Preparation

The product leader needs to start at an early stage in the company's existence with preparation. The things to prepare are a mirror of the items I listed in Chapter 14 that are typically included in a buy-side diligence engagement:

Licenses and Intellectual Property

Track any commercial and open source licenses in use. It's also a good practice to have a policy across Engineering to enforce the types of licenses that are allowed and which ones require leadership sign-off. If you publish open source as a company, you should also have a practice or policy to follow a set of standards and make sure libraries and license types are approved by engineering leadership and Legal—mainly to make sure that you aren't exposing any business or technical IP and that proper licenses are in place. You also want to track all contributions to your internal IP and make sure that employees and contracts all have signed releases in place.

Privacy and Data Governance

Companies are increasingly using data throughout their business, and with the rapidly changing privacy laws, companies need to be aware of how data is acquired, used, and stored. If you are involved in a complex data business, you definitely want to create a detailed data map and keep it updated as you scale the business. It needs to include the following attributes for each data source the company is responsible for: acquisition process (mapped to user consent policies); whether the data is public, private, or confidential; where and how it is stored and transmitted (type of encryption and physical security); the lifecycle/retention policies; and governance—or what products it is used in and how it can be used. This last point is really critical and important to enforce and document. Just because data is sitting around in the business doesn't mean it can be used in a new product idea. You have to tie the data consent by the user to the way it is being used in the product (can this data be used only in aggregate or anonymously, can it be exported to a third party, etc.?). A business that is lax about how they track and manage data can quickly get a number of products in market that are valuable and lead to an acquisition opportunity only to have it crushed when they realize they are using data inappropriately or illegally.

Security

Document your security policy (in coordination with your SecOps team) and show how secure practices are used in system design and development. Have a security diagram for your network and systems and track the entry points and the individuals with access. You'll also want a document that details how training is done and what controls are in place for determining and limiting employee access to systems or tools that provide access to customer data. For example: Do customers have to allow an account manager to access their data through internal tools, or can any employee access it whenever? Do engineers have access to production data or just operation team members? And is that full-time access or leased team when there are system issues? You also want to log access to production systems and be able to report and track this. Finally, make sure to document any security breaches and any penetration testing and results.

Product

For early products, document the discovery process and path to product/market fit. For mature products, track the customer usage data. You'll also want to show recent product enhancements, what drove those decisions, and the current breakdown of time spent on new innovation, feature enhancements, and maintenance. It's also important to keep an updated long-term roadmap and resource allocation document that shows the individuals and teams working on various products across the organization.

Documenting Systems and Processes

I like to keep an up-to-date system diagram that serves as an internal design document for engineering, but also can be used for security reviews, audits, and diligence. It's also important to track project work and be able to report on the flow of a reported bug on a support ticket, through a product management Agile tool, to deployment in production. This process is important to show during diligence, but also as the company gets larger for audits.

Metrics

Tracking systems and product usage metrics are important for any business. Make sure to focus on uptime metrics and long-term tracking of customer impacting events—especially if the company has any service-level agreements in place.

Costs

This includes detailed costs around running the product development organization. Breakdowns on people/system costs per product are really interesting to show investment and return. On the system side, it is important to show fixed and variable costs around licenses and SaaS tools, as well as hosting/data-center costs and the historic and projected cost curve.

16

Selling Your Company

Telling the Story

Next to being prepared, you need to be able to tell a great story about where the business is at—and specifically, how the product development organization is doing. We just defined the building blocks of a great story above in the preparation part in Chapter 15, so your job is to weave this data together in a way that tells the story of the product evolution up to the current success of the product in market. The story will of course detail the processes that you have implemented that make sense for the stage of growth for the company. More importantly, you should be able to describe the processes that you are planning to implement that aren't in place yet. This presents the business in the best light and builds confidence that the leadership team knows exactly where to go, but is being practical and iterative in getting there. It also presents risk up front instead of the buyer digging in and finding things that are a surprise to the process.

Other than being able to walk through the data, processes that are in place, and the risk, the product and engineering leaders' key job is to sell the value of the product and the team. Assuming you have a great product that has found product-market fit and is scaling well, you should be able to talk about the current value, ROI, future roadmap, projected growth, and know enough about the buyer to articulate how the product fits into their overall strategic plan. Similarly, for the team. If you've spent time creating a great culture and efficient team operating system that is innovative, executing well, and hitting outcomes, then showcase that and show how this team is key for the deal.

In the second edition of *Startup CEO*, Matt tells the story of a failed sale process at Return Path. We received an unsolicited inbound offer from a large company and while we had some preparation in place from the list in Chapter 15, we hadn't done enough. The weeks-long diligence process was exhaustive and wore us out. The process was highly confidential and we were trying to keep the internal team small so it created a lot of work for us. The day before the scheduled signing of the definitive agreement, the buyer got cold feet. The deal was off. We felt crushed, not just because the deal was dead, but because the core members of the team responsible for telling the story of the business had failed. Ultimately the reason the deal failed was because of a number of risk elements that the acquiring company felt were too much for them to absorb and integrate.

We had complex international data privacy agreements and a large technical organization that was in the middle of a big reinvention, migrating to the cloud from data centers, and tackling GDPR. Sometimes you can get prepared for a sale and tell a perfectly good story about where the business is at, but the timing is wrong. However, this was also a big lesson on how to communicate risks to an acquiring company. While we were transparent and clear about the stage the business was at and all of the work we were doing, it came across looking like more than we could handle on our timetable and contributed to the risk. The key lesson is that you have to tell both sides of the risk story—be transparent about the work and the risk, but also sell your team and their creativity, resilience, and historical performance at being able to solve big problems. It turns out that our team was successful in reinventing the business, migrating to the cloud, and handling GDPR on the schedule we proposed. We were also very prepared for the next opportunity to handle an incoming offer, and eventually a successful exit to Validity in 2019.

III. CTO/CPO AND THE LEADERSHIP TEAM

17

How to Hire a Chief Technology Officer

Shawn Nussbaum

Earlier in the book (Chapter 4) we wrote about product development leaders and stated that the most senior technical person should be a leader, but that doesn't mean that the Technology Officer has to be the strongest programmer because that's not what a leader does. The role of the CTO leader is to communicate deep technical details to internal and external business stakeholders, to grow a leadership team and effectively manage people, and to understand how to use technology as a strategic asset to help the business succeed. We also said that our best success in developing leaders is to do that internally, to widen the funnel to bring in diverse talent, to develop product team-specific onboarding processes, and to develop career paths for technical contributors. But for a lot of startups and scaleups, developing your own technical leaders is just not possible. Either you don't have enough runway to develop people, or maybe the task is too difficult for your existing people, or sometimes you have a CTO exit unexpectedly. For companies facing these situations, an outside chief technology officer might be your only option. I am using the concept of *personas* applied to the CTO role.

We wrote this book with a broad approach to product / technology, merging everything that has to do with designing, developing, and operating software products as a whole team under the label "product." But your own organization could be more segmented than that and you could have a CPO, a CTO, or both. This chapter focuses on how to hire a CTO because, even though the CPO and CTO roles are similar, they differ in significant ways and you can't just use the CPO framework to hire your CTO. Earlier, (Chapter 4) Scott Petry wrote in his textbox that the CPO is often driven by "why" and the CTO is driven by "how," and while that might be true on some grand scale, in reality the CPO and CTO differ in more nuanced ways.

Persona Attributes and How to Find Them

For the CTO role there are three *personas,* a technical leader, a team leader, and a strategy leader. The technical leader is often a cofounder and provides thought leadership externally. This person understands the competitive landscape, both narrowly in the specifics of the market where the organization competes, and more broadly understands the competitive landscape of tangential products. Typically, the technical leader is the strongest technologist in the organization and they shape the long-term technical vision and lead the architecture. The technical leader stays up to date on the technical landscape through research, development, and new tooling and they often are involved in prototyping advancements, whether alone or within a "CTO Office" populated with architects or research engineers. On LinkedIn or another platform, you will find the technical leader as a person who highlights startup and tech cofounder experience, or a person who provides details on scaling technology (rather than scaling teams), or provides details about deep product innovation.

The team leader CTO will also be highly technical and will contribute to technological advancement in the early stages of the company, but their true skill is that they are a great manager and team builder. As a manager, the team leader will lead day-to-day execution, they will help to build the organizational structure, reporting lines, and team composition of the engineering process, and they will be highly involved in the planning process, including prioritizing features and products and ensuring releases deliver on time. They bring vision for the engineering organization and will address and resolve team issues. The team leader is a strong recruiter helping to build the engineering culture and maintain morale. As a highly involved leader in all aspects of engineering, the team leader is able to easily navigate the chaos of building products. On LinkedIn or another platform, a team leader will highlight startup and scale experience, often providing details about scaling that include team structure, organizational change, and recruiting and hiring. The team leader might also provide details about delivering products, and the planning, processes, releases and capacity planning required to do that effectively.

The strategy leader CTO is more likely to be found in an organization that is scaling rapidly, or already more mature than a startup. The strategy leader will own the technical strategy for the business and can articulate (and defend) a business plan on how technology can be used as a force-multiplier for the business. They will have a deep understanding of budgeting and financial impacts of technical and team decisions both in the short-term and also in long-term planning. A strategy leader will be comfortable working with multiple teams and engineers in a multiprod-uct strategy where the responsibility for shipping cohesive products falls to single threaded leaders. Because of their strategic focus, the strategy leader CTO will be instrumental in driving innovation and efficiency. On LinkedIn or another platform, the strategy leader CTO will highlight their large-stage company experience in scaling teams, their work on deep organizational change and technical scale projects, and provide evidence of driving innovation and efficiency at scale.

When is The Right Time For This *Persona?*

The *personas* identified are not interchangeable and there are specific reasons, based on the growth stage and complexity of your company, that will inform *when* to hire your next CTO. If you're thinking about a technical leader CTO, a good time to consider someone with that person is if you have an early-stage technical cofounder who is responsible for building an MVP. If you are at the growth stage a technical leader CTO can be a good choice, especially if you need to scale out the system and evolve the product. There are also certain mature companies that are deeply technical who could use a technical leader CTO if, for example, they need a hands-on leader to help continue to drive the technical vision, to experiment, or to innovate new products.

A team leader CTO would be a good hire for a growth-stage company where the initial team is getting large enough that direction and management are needed by a dedicated people leader. If you find that your company is at the point where the business needs a more efficient or effective engineering process, or if you find that during your scaling you need to hire someone quickly to coordinate a number of teams, a team leader can be very helpful.

A strategy leader should be considered when you need a business leader who has a deep technical/product background to manage a complex product organization, drive a big impact at the executive/board level, or navigate complex organizational change.

General Interview Questions

There are several general questions that can be helpful in interviewing CTO candidates.

- Where do you spend most of your time? Road-mapping/ strategy, managing your team? In the weeds on the technology?

- Are you still technical/ how hands on are you? Do you code? (unlikely) or make architecture decisions/architecture reviews?

- What do you own? Development, QA, infrastructure? (Maybe a better way to ask that is- what do you NOT own?)

- How big is your team? Are they centralized or distributed?

- What areas of the stack are you strongest?

- Can you give me an example of a major product or a launch that was behind schedule yet your team managed to ship on time? How did you accomplish this?

- Tell me the best way to organize an engineering team at an early stage company?

- How have you been most successful hiring in such a competitive market?

- How do you motivate/incentivize your teams? What is your management philosophy?

- How do you align development, QA, and product, since these groups sometimes are driven by their own objectives? How do you create an environment where all work effectively together and for a common goal?

- Where do you thrive most:

  - Environments where you're taking something more legacy and are driving innovation/reinvention?

  - Or an environment where things are constantly changing and you need to create a vision to build something new from the ground up (startup)?

Questions For Each *Persona*

Finally, there are questions you can ask each candidate but you ought to expect different answers based on their *persona*. For example, if you ask the question, "Where do you spend most of your time: strategy, managing teams, or on the technology?" a technical leader will most likely reply that they spend time on technical things, like innovation and strategy. A team leader would respond that they spend time their team, recruiting and hiring people, planning and delivery. While a strategy leader, with their strategy focus will spend time on large-scale problems and change management.

If you ask each candidate, "What motivates you more: driving innovation/reinvention at scale or managing constant change at an early-stage company and creating a vision and building something from scratch?" a technology leader would likely respond that at an early stage company they are motivated to build technology from scratch, while at scale they are motivated to scale technology and generate iterative innovation. A team leader will be motivated to build teams, either from scratch at an early stage company or scaling them at a more mature company. The strategy leader, most likely to be motivated to join a company at scale, would likely answer that their motivation is driving innovation and reinvention at scale.

It's also helpful to get a sense of what KPIs each candidate tracks against and here, too, you ought to expect different responses for each *persona*. If you ask the question, "What KPIs do you typically track against?" the technical leader will often respond, system KPIs, product KPIs, balance of technical versus feature work. The team leader will track against engineering cycle time, recruiting and hiring pipeline, and product KPIs and the strategy leader will track against team KPIs, cost, and product KPIs.

While you may think of the CPO and CTO roles as interchangeable, our advice is to think deeply about your organization, your stage of growth, complexity, and values, to find the right person to lead your product / technology teams. A wrong approach is to focus exclusively on the skills and experience of candidates without considering your company dynamics. By using the *personas* framework you will be able to at least whittle down the vast number of candidates to a manageable few and from there you can use the questions above as guidelines to make your next CTO hire a success.

How to Hire a Chief Product Officer

Shawn Nussbaum

One way to approach hiring for the CPO role is to think about the skills and attributes a person will bring with them and rather than pore over resumes and details of every possible candidate, we have found that there are three distinct *personas* that define the vast majority of product development leaders. The three *personas,* what we call visionary, executor, and general manager, are relatively distinct and cohesive so that people in one *persona* will be similar to all others in that *persona* but different from people in the other *personas.* By the time you get to the CPO level, you are obviously familiar with the many different flavors of product development, but each person will have preferences, values, and deeper experience in one *persona* rather than deep experience in all of them. Choosing the right CPO for your startup depends on finding a person with the *persona* that will make a big impact moving forward for your company and specific situation.

Persona Attributes and How to Find Them

As you would expect, a visionary CPO excels at formulating and articulating a vision and relies on the vision as a way to gain buy-in with the product team and others in the organization. A visionary will want ownership of the vision and will thrive when the founder/CEO is not a product visionary. That is, the visionary will fill that void but to do that they will need autonomy. They will also find the most joy in shipping beautiful end-user products and to do that they will gravitate toward being data-informed rather than data-driven and analytical. One caution on bringing in a visionary CPO: if the CEO is strongly product-led then the visionary CPO and CEO will most likely clash. This is not an issue if you have a company that values debate, differing opinions, and sees conflict as a key to making great decisions. But if your company values cohesiveness over conflict, a visionary might not be the best choice for you because it could lead to distractions and delays in decision-making.

If you are looking for a visionary and using a platform like LinkedIn, another platform, or an executive recruiter, look for people who were involved with a startup or has cofounder experience. If you can't find that, then someone with deep product innovation experience, or experience reinventing legacy products will tend to be more visionary in their approach.

The executor *persona* differs from the visionary in several significant ways. For example, the executor will tend to thrive with a product-led CEO and will be able to translate the founder's (or CEO's) vision to product strategy. The executor is very strong around optimizing, scaling, process, urgency, and team development. They will be excellent communicators and can inspire people at all levels of a company. One caution in hiring an executor CPO is that they may have aspirations to be COO, so you'll have to determine their career goals to see if they fit your needs. It would be disruptive to bring in an executor CPO who exits after a short stint leaving you to go through the whole hiring process again. On LinkedIn or another platform, a person with startup or cofounder experience may fit the executor *persona,* or someone who highlights experience and details around process and KPIs. You may also find people who tend to be executors if they highlight details about market-fit and scaling.

The third *persona* that you're likely to encounter for a CPO role is the General Manager, or GM. This person will have very strong business acumen, and strong preferences for cross-functional collaboration. They will want to tie business strategy to product strategy and their leadership preference is to work to build strong alignment with GTM functions and bridge both internal and external stakeholders. The GM will be more focused on metrics and data and less focused on the look and feel of a product but they will understand the competitive landscape very well and will know where to go, how to win, and what market dynamics and customer targets to go after. On LinkedIn or another platform, look for someone who has large-stage company experience, or experience scaling product teams. You may also find people who have the GM *persona* who list skills around deep organizational change.

When is the Right Time For This *Persona*?

Once you have identified which *persona* is best for your CPO hire your next task is to figure out when in the growth journey of your company you should hire this person. While there are no hard and fast rules, in general you would want to hire a visionary CPO during your early stage with the mandate to be a product cofounder. If you are at a later stage then a visionary CPO can be very effective in reinventing a legacy product. If you have a gap within your company around vision, if the founder / CEO isn't a product visionary, then bringing in a visionary CPO can be very helpful. If you are beyond the startup stage and you have a big brand, you are B2C, or you have a deeply innovative product, a visionary CPO can sometimes be a very good fit.

The executor CPO can also be a good choice for a startup or a company in the early stages of growth, especially if the founder / CEO is a product visionary. The executor will be able to balance the visionary tendency of the founder / CEO and can be a cofounder / partner. The executor CPO also works well when a company has scaled because of their skills and preferences for process, optimizing, and team development. The GM CPO works best if a company is at scale, is more mature, and if it is complex with multi-line products and multiple stakeholders. With their strong business acumen and preference for collaboration with GTM and other teams, and their knowledge of metrics and data, the GM CPO works well with larger complex companies.

General Interview Questions

Although three *personas* were identified that ought to serve you well in hiring your first (or next) CPO, there are some general questions you can ask each CPO candidate.

- Do you own all __'s products? (Will help you get a sense for the way the org is structured and how broad their role is)

- What did the product/product organization look like when you joined? Where are your fingerprints? (Will help you get a sense for growth and also help you understand what they have actually built)

- What does your team look like today? What is the makeup of your team? (Can also prompt with, are you managing Product Managers, engineering, QA, UX, designers? Etc.)

- How close are you to development? Managing engineers?

- What type of products are you building? Infrastructure/platform, platform at the application layer, content engines, consumer internet/website, etc.?

Questions For Each *Persona*

If you are unsure about a person's *persona,* there are questions you can ask where you would expect different answers. For example, if you ask the question, "What part of Product do you own/influence? What stakeholders do you collaborate with?" A visionary would most likely respond "all of it," because a visionary is more externally focused and motivated. A visionary would also respond that they are likely to collaborate most closely with the CEO and they expect to report to the CEO. An executor, responding to that question, might say that the founder/CEO owns the product vision and the executor's role is to partner with the founder on product strategy. The executor, unlike the visionary, is more likely to be internally focused. Finally, the GM may respond that they own the P&L for certain product lines and that they would expect tight integration and influence with internal stakeholders.

Another question that will help differentiate the three *personas* is, "What motivates you more: driving innovation/reinvention at scale or managing constant change at an early-stage company and creating a vision and building something from scratch?" For a visionary you should expect to hear that they are motivated to build a product from scratch and get it to product-market fit. An executor will also be motivated to build a product from scratch, but as a partner to a founding team. While the GM will be more motivated to lead a product at scale or build out a team of product managers to run products at scale.

A final question to ask each *persona,* is, "What KPIs do you typically track against?" Here you ought to expect three different answers. The visionary might track against customer-facing metrics and business success; the executor will track against business success and product usage; and the GM will track business success, team development and performance, and financials.

As mentioned, you can have great success with building product development teams and coaching and mentoring internal candidates to become the CPO, but recognize that an internal approach is not always practical or feasible for every company. If you have to hire a CPO, using the *personas* as a guideline or framework will help you understand candidates better so that you can find the CPO who will excel in the role. The CPO needs to be in the room when the big business decisions get made and they can't let the team just be the technical arm of a company that is handed specifications to go build. They have to ensure that Product Development is integral to the business and they do that by setting the product vision and strategy to execute. While all three *personas* will be capable of that, there are nuances that you should consider given your company's stage of growth. That is, they need to help set the product vision and strategy and execute Product Development across the organization in collaboration with internal and external business stakeholders.

19

How I Work With the Leadership Team

Shawn Nussbaum

At both Return Path and Bolster we have always had the perspective that your first team is the leadership team. The responsibility for everyone on the leadership team is to see and identify with their peers at the executive level. That not only means that you need to spend as much time with the leadership team as you do with your functional team, but it also means that the leadership meetings are where the collaboration and decision making happens. That is where the deep problems and conflicts are solved so that what gets translated down to your own functional area will lead to effective participation by the rest of the organization.

The team first concept is very different from what happens in a lot of companies, where the leadership team defends their turf and competes with each other. So many corporations are bureaucratic and hierarchical and their leadership meetings consist of discussions where people defend and make the case for the marketing team or the product team or the sales team to the CEO and to their peers. It's a challenging dynamic where the senior leaders are protecting their turf and they are more responsible to the people in their departments than they are to trying to find solutions and be collaborative at the executive level. Even somebody who describes themselves as a "collaborative executive" will often be talking about how they work effectively with their team downline rather than talking about how they collaborated with their peer executives.

In thinking about how I work with my peers on the executive team I do that through the first team lens. From both a technical standpoint and a product standpoint, the most important thing that the role brings to the leadership team is helping them understand that technology or a product can be a force multiplier for the business. As the CTO/CPO you are in a unique position to help your peers understand that product isn't just assembly line work. There are a lot of companies that treat the product team as order-takers, where they make decisions and the product team will just stamp out the cookie cutter shapes that the executives decided they're going to sell. Companies that operate this way miss the value of an effective head of product or head of technology because that person can define an innovative process that will become the core asset of the company. Product is not just something that is stamped out in an assembly line but is something that is deeply creative in what a company is known for, especially in technology or product enabled companies. So one way to work effectively with the leadership team is helping them understand that force multiplier effect, defining that, and being responsible for it.

The second way that a CTO/CPO can work effectively with the leadership team is in helping to manage that impedance mismatch that I referred to in Chapter 13. The product organization has a roadmap and is delivering things incrementally but other parts of the organization, like marketing or sales, might be very event-driven. They have a conference coming up, what can they ship? They have a hard deadline but product is focused on testing ideas and being incremental, so there is an impedance mismatch. My role is to translate that mismatch, to share with the leadership team that product operates a certain way to build a product that's innovative and that process of creativity requires its own timeline. It's iterative because we are trying to figure out what the customer wants and evolve that.

What I try to communicate to the rest of my peers on the leadership team is that, just because you need another widget in the bag to sell, that doesn't mean that we go and build that product or add that product to drive sales. The product holistically has to stand on its own and the process that product uses is different than the rest of running the business. My role isn't to be an order-taker but to create value and try to figure out what the customer wants.

As a startup CTO/CPO working with the leadership team is critical. Having a mindset (and practices around) a team first perspective and being aware of impedance mismatches and managing around them will make a long-term impact in the business.

20

Fractional Chief Product/Technology Officer

Drew Dillon

Getting Started in a Fractional Product Role

A lot of people in Product have a random resumé where it's a little bit of sales, a little bit of engineering, a little bit of design, and then all of sudden you're in Product because if you average all those together you've basically defined "product." When I first spoke with CEOs I was often the first person that the CEO had ever met who did a product fractional job. They really had no idea what I did or how they could work with me; I was just a person that their VC told them they needed to talk to. For product and technology roles there are two hurdles to overcome because you have to sell your role and then sell yourself on top of it. The term "fractional" changed all that and takes a lot of guesswork off the table. Maybe a company doesn't need me five days a week, maybe just a couple of days a week. I'll come in, we'll work together, and maybe it will be a full-time gig or maybe we'll get to this good spot and I'll help them find a full-time leader.

I would suggest anyone considering a fractional role to not leave their full-time job until they at least have a couple of people interested in hiring them. Making fractional work sustainable is less about the first round of leads and it's really about the next round. So, planning for that period when that first set of contracts ends you need to be able to answer the question, how are you going to get that next set of folks? What's your unique value? And how do you brand what you do in a way that's really easy for a company to hire you?

I had a friend who was doing engineering and CTO work and he suggested starting by writing a blog post and say exactly what I am going to do. Then, when people ask, "What do you do?" I sent them the link to a fairly tactical blog post with a menu of items to choose from. That worked great for me, and later I followed up with a blog post on scaling product strategy which highlighted how I help companies at various points in their lifecycle. When you're first getting into this, it's nearly impossible to describe exactly what your benefit is going to be for a company and so writing the blog post forced me to be concrete and explicit. It also forced me to outline some broad challenges that startups and scaleups face, like every company at some point faces a gap in product leadership. That's something that resonates with lots of founders so from there I needed to help people see that I could not only fill that gap but help them accelerate through it.

What Does a Fractional Product Person Do?

There's probably a lot of ways to work with companies but I usually work in three areas. The first one is like a Think Tank where they will give me a lot of information and I'll go conduct some research and come back with results, data, and my thoughts on their questions. The second way I work with companies is as a coach to the executive and I will participate in their executive meetings and facilitate longer-term planning. And a third way is to help build a product team and help interview and recruit a full-time replacement. The third way is actually a true fractional role and I lead the function as though I were a full-time employee and help hire my full-time replacement.

One thing that a fractional executive does, or should do, is to be honest about what they see. I charge by the project so I'm not obsessed with the hours—I don't need a company to keep me on for 12 months. So, I'm going to give them the best answer I possibly can to help their business because I feel that's ultimately what they're hiring me for. Even if it's tough advice, they're going to get that advice and they're going to hear the truth and hear what I think. Some people tell a client what they want to hear or they want to raise issues or problems so they can stick around and bill more hours. My perspective as a fractional is just the opposite: I give you the straight truth and my goal is to bring my best to the company so that they can move forward.

Advice for Companies

If you're considering a person to come in and help your company, one of the key differences between a fractional role and a consulting or advising role is that you really need the fractional person to own the function. While a lot of people might have the skills, a fractional person is someone who will make a much bigger impact in your company because they'll work closely with your team, technology, and markets. One way to screen for that is to look for curiosity. How curious is a person about the problem? Are they really getting in there and learning about your challenges? Are they really going to get their hands dirty and help you with the problem? Or do they give you solutions quickly, like they have a solution and they're looking for problems?

One thing I find in working with companies, especially startups, is that they can't pin down exactly what they need so they should think about precisely what they're looking for. If it has something to do with product and a company can't pin it down, they should at least be able to come up with some broad categories, like it's a strategic project, or it's writing specs, or it's someone to come in and focus the product team, or we need someone to help the executive and management teams. I worked with a company once where they said, "We don't know what we don't know. We don't know whether we need you to execute. We don't know whether we need you to tell us what we're doing. But what we want to know is what having somebody like you around will do for us. We need to know what having an executive product voice is within our company so we can know whether to hire a person." In that case, I helped them calibrate what level of help they needed. So, even if a company doesn't know what they need, a fractional person can still be helpful.

Another thing, and this might be specific to product or technology, is that we operate in a space that is unique to the core DNA of a company. I initially thought that there wouldn't be a need for a fractional executive because the founders or someone close to the business wouldn't see a need for help in this area, or that they wouldn't be open to an outsider coming in and understanding their core technology.

I haven't found that to be a problem and instead I get all sorts of input from founders as to how they feel about that. Some of them will come back with, "Well, we put a lot of effort into training people and we don't want to put that money into you because as a fractional you'll leave." That's a genuine concern but my usual response is that if a company feels like they need to put a lot of money into training me, then I'm not very good at my job.

The other thing that I wondered about was whether or not the existing team would connect with me, especially whether engineers would work with a product person. Would they see me as a threat or as a person who wanted to help them? From what I've seen, as long as the morale of the company isn't shot, as long as there isn't broad mistrust in the company, then people are going to give you the benefit of the doubt that you're being brought in as an expert. Obviously, your experience matters here because it gives you credibility in the game, but after the initial introductions, it's all about how you operate and work with the team. My first discussions with people are around the challenges they're seeing and as they describe them I can say, "Oh, I wrote something on that." And because I've written those blog posts and put my ideas out there, people know that I understand and care about their concerns.

They will often say, "Yes, he really does get engineering, or data science, or he really does have a philosophy on product."

Final Thought

One other thing I haven't mentioned yet is that this is just a lot of fun. I was interviewing some candidates for a VP of Product for a company and at the end of the conversation I asked them if they had any questions and their main question was, "How do you get to do what you do?" That pretty much sums it up: interesting work, great people, new challenges, the ability to help people, and tons of fun.

21

CEO-to-CEO Advice About the Technology / Product Role

Matt Blumberg

What comes before a full-fledged Chief Product or Technology Officer? In most startups, this role is played by one or more founders. Sometimes it is engineering-focused, sometimes it is a product visionary, sometimes it is both in one role, and sometimes it is two roles. Because of that, I'll address each role separately here.

Signs It's Time to Hire Your First Chief Product Officer

You know it's time to hire a Chief Product Officer when:

- You wake up in the middle of the night and realize that your product vision has gotten stale because your leadership of it has had to take a back seat to other issues around running the company or fundraising.

- You are spending too much of your own time managing the connectivity between Engineering and Product Management relative to the connectivity between product and go-to-market.

- Your Board asks you what the long-term roadmap is, and you don't have a great answer and aren't sure how to get to one.

When a Fractional Chief Product Officer Might Be Enough

A fractional Chief Product Officer may be the way to go if you have solid mid-level product management leadership but need extra experience to dig into product-market fit issues and create a new high level roadmap, or even to lay out a new process for creating that roadmap.

Signs It's Time to Hire Your First Chief Technology Officer

You know it's time to hire a Chief Technology Officer when:

- You wake up in the middle of the night worrying about a potential system outage.

- You are spending too much of your own time thinking about technical debt, engineering throughput, and security issues or audits.

- Your Board asks you what your Business Continuity Plan is, and you don't have a great answer and aren't sure how to get to one.

When a Fractional Chief Technology Officer Might Be Enough

A fractional Chief Technology Officer may be the way to go if your Engineering leader is a very strong coder and troubleshooter who needs some mentorship to become a strong architect and cultural leader.

What Does Great Look Like in a Chief Product or Technology Officer?

Ideal startup Chief Product or Technology Officers do three things particularly well:

1. They create product by starting with the business objective, not the technology. Even the most hardcore technology enthusiast in the world can't produce the best product by starting with technology. The selection of platforms, languages, databases, and architecture must fit the needs of the business and customers and available workforce, not the other way around.

2. They know the balance of taking shortcuts to get things to market quickly AND going back and cleaning up the shortcuts methodically after the fact. Shawn's whole point in this Part about "scrappy, not crappy" was a phrase that drove us over the last few years at Return Path. No one wants to get things into the hands of customers faster than a typical startup CEO. No CEO will ever get equally fired up about paying down technical debt. Great heads of Product, Technology, Engineering must be the standard bearers for this.

3. They are deeply concerned about the culture and career paths within the product or engineering organizations. In most technology companies, the two largest groups of employees are Sales and Product. In consumer-facing technology companies, the sin-

gle largest is usually Product and, specifically, Engineering. The leader who knows how to optimize for engagement and retention, who spends real time thinking about compensation bands and career paths, who mentors engineers and trains them to be principal engineers or managers—that's the leader who knows how to get the most out of the team. There is also a role for the strong senior engineer who focuses only on the code or only on the development process—but that is probably not the person you want to rely on as your main executive in charge of the whole of the department unless they have a superb #2 who is almost a co-leader, or who knows how to partner very effectively with your Head of People.

Signs Your Chief Product or Technology Officer Isn't Scaling

Chief Product or Technology Officers who aren't scaling well past the startup stage are the ones who typically:

- Focus and thrive on individual contributor work like bug/code troubleshooting or pulling all-nighters on coding or releases. Similar to Sales, where you have a problem when your CRO gets more excited about closing a deal than with a rep closing a deal, Product leaders need to be focused on building the overall product machine, not on writing code. If what Bill Gates says is true—that the best engineer is 10x more productive than the average engineer—and I believe that to be true, then companies need to reward that engineer with a generous compensation package, not with a senior executive role, unless the engineer promises to make everyone else 10x as productive!

- Are not interested in engaging with sales reps and customers. Even the most introverted engineer can figure out how to do this in ways that aren't incredibly uncomfortable, like sitting in the back of the room at every user group or listening to sales calls on Gong. Even better to be an executive sponsor on a key account or speak at a customer conference.

- Downplay advice from nontechnical CEO or leaders because "they don't understand the technology." This is a bright red flag, and one that you only need to see once as a CEO. It's bad enough when advice on product from a nontechnical CEO is rejected, but it's even worse when the same happens with advice on other things like employee matters or interpersonal issues between executives. If you have a nontechnical CEO who respects and gives you a lot of leeway on technical matters, pay attention to the things they question or offer up. They may have some good insights because they're further away from the technology. Heads of Product or Engineering are clearly in trouble when they use this argument as a way of not doing something that someone outside their organization notices and suggests.

How I Engage with the Chief Product or Technology Officer

A few ways I've typically spent the most time with or gotten the most value out of Chief Product or Technology Officers over the years are:

- Challenging a paradigm shift. Years ago, when our business at Return Path started to take off and our CTO was thinking about how to scale 1.5x in the coming year, I challenged him to think about what he would do if we had 10x increase in volume. After his head stopped exploding, he began to think very differently about how to scale some of the trickier aspects of our system architecture. That led to a really different plan, and an outcome of a more efficient system, in the short term, that we might not otherwise have experienced.

- Bringing business strategy and acumen into the product team. Our various product leaders always asked me to do dedicated roundtable sessions with their leadership teams to riff on the business. Although these meetings were usually unstructured, product leaders always came with massive amounts of questions and opinions about the company. At Return Path anyway, they were more inquisitive about some of the ins and outs of strategy and finance than other teams, and these conversations almost always resulted in some new ideas for our product roadmap that made them worthwhile.

- Applying learnings from Product to the rest of the organization. Engineers are trained to think differently than most other people in the company, so they frequently think up new ways to do things that others might never come up with. At Return Path, our CTO was the one who came up with the idea to create a structured return-to-work program for moms who had taken a career break to raise kids. He was dogged in his pursuit of the concept. We funded and nurtured it, and it attracted national attention and grew to the point where we spun it out into a new nonprofit company called Path Forward. I'm not sure if we would have dreamed that up without a systems thinker pushing it. The out-of-the-box thinking by the CTO is a great example of "Agile Everywhere."

22

Conclusion

Leading a product development organization is a challenging and rewarding job and really is the intersection of technology, business, and people. We want to conclude this Part by reiterating the core foundational items to get right to build an effective product development organization and scale it as the company grows.

The role of product development leadership is not just to be the execution arm of the business but to be an integral part of the business, setting and communicating product strategy, connecting other business functions together around a shared vision, and using technology as a force-multiplier and strategic asset for the business. Success is measured not by the output from Product Development, but by hitting outcomes.

The right culture is key to cultivating the type of environment that allows people to have ownership, a deep understanding of the business, influence on outcomes, freedom to experiment, and a place to innovate and create remarkable products. Effective teams are diverse teams that are psychologically safe and empower people to trust, make mistakes, and do their best work.

Build a product development organization that is aligned with the business and has a culture of solving business problems with Engineering, not just solving engineering problems. A proportional product development approach maximizes effectiveness and scales with the business as it grows.

Acknowledgements

This book is derivative of Startup CXO and the acknowledgments for this book extends to the people who helped in that effort. The list of people to thank for their role in helping create that is long and has to start with my current and former colleagues who were the primary contributors: Jack Sinclair, Cathy Hawley, Shawn Nussbaum, Ken Takahashi, Nick Badgett, Holly Enneking, Anita Absey, George Bilbrey, Dennis Dayman, and Dave Wilby. Startup CXO was a truly collaborative work and the same is true with this book. Shawn and I collaborated together and also with Pete Birkeland, who edited the second edition of Startup CEO, was a tireless collaborator for Startup CXO, and helped bring this book to fruition.

I would also like to acknowledge the rest of the Bolster team and board that made this possible, especially this book's project manager, Rachel Henry. It wasn't easy to carve out the time to write while scaling up Bolster, much less doing the bulk of the writing over the holidays and I'm grateful to all the contributors for their effort.

Although the professional lives of the contributors are now primarily at Bolster, most of us worked together for many years at Return Path, and all of us would like to thank our Board and shareholders, particularly Fred Wilson, Greg Sands, Scott Weiss, Scott Petry, Jeff Epstein, and Brad Feld (more on Brad in a minute) for giving us the opportunity to learn on the job as we scaled ourselves and scaled the business over the better part of two decades. That experience is what led us to be able to write Startup CXO. We'd also like to thank all 1,300 colleagues from Return Path over the years who challenged, inspired, and taught us things every day. Although he was not a Return Path or Bolster team member, Marc Maltz from Hoola Hoop Consulting, my long-time partner as an executive coach, has shaped the thinking of me and of a number of the contributors to this effort.

Startup CXO is part of the Startup Revolution series that was created by my long-time board member and friend Brad Feld. Brad's advice on all things business, personal, and writing has been invaluable for over 20 years and whether attributed or not, many of the ideas in this book are the result of many thoughtful conversations with him. I would also like to thank the team at Wiley (Bill Falloon and Purvi Patel) for their help and support as editors, publishers, and marketers.

Startup CXO had a very large number of people who contributed their insights to the final form, which carries over to this book, including sidebars by Rob Krolik and Jeff Epstein, Guy Turner, Greg Sands, Scott Petry, Brad Feld, Dave Wilby, and Scott Dorsey. We are also grateful for the contribution to our fractional chapter from Drew Dillon.

We received a number of thoughtful comments on specific functional areas from Rick Buck, Caroline Pearl, Diana Caleroni, Jen Goldman, Mike Mutone, Debby Meredith, and Chad Shinsato. Brad Feld and Scott Dorsey did a final read-through of the entire book (not a small feat!) and provided helpful suggestions to the final work.

I want to end by thanking my family for their unwavering support as I embarked on a series of books while scaling a second startup—a combination that I can't exactly endorse as being sane or smart. Startup CXO was a collaborative effort but I would have been the anchor holding us back if it weren't for my wife of over two decades, Mariquita. My thanks start and end with her. An executive coach for startup CEOs, Mariquita has been intimately involved in all my professional projects, providing advice, encouragement, and support to whatever I'm doing.

Matt Blumberg

About the Authors

Matt Blumberg. Matt Blumberg. Matt has spent his entire career creating startups, scaling them, and sharing best practices of what works and what doesn't work for other CEOs and team members in the entrepreneurial community. He is the author of *Startup CEO: A Field Guide to Scaling Up Your Business* (Wiley, 2020), an influential book embraced by entrepreneurs, CEOs, founders, and board of directors in the entrepreneurial ecosystem. *Startup CEO* was an outgrowth of his blog, StartupCEO.com. In 1999, he founded Return Path, an innovative email marketing company, helped it to $100m in revenues, and led it to a successful exit in a strategic sale to Validity in 2019. Along with colleagues from Return Path, Matt started Bolster in 2020, a company focused on helping startups and scaleups grow, develop, and scale their leadership teams and boards. Matt's second book, *Startup CXO: A Field Guide to Scaling Up Your Company's Critical Functions and Teams* (Wiley, 2021), was a collaboration with Bolster's CXOs to provide a blueprint for scaling up each function.

Before Return Path, Matt led Marketing, Product Management, and the Internet Group for MovieFone, Inc. (later acquired by AOL). Prior to that, he served as an associate with private equity firm General Atlantic Partners and was a consultant with Mercer Management Consulting. He also cofounded and chairs the board of Path Forward, a nonprofit created and spun out of Return Path. Path Forward's mission is to empower people to restart their careers after time spent focused on caregiving by working with companies offering mid-career internships. Path Forward gives women and men a path to a professional career, while giving companies access to a diverse, untapped talent force. Matt is currently Executive Chair at Bolster. He earned his A.B. from Princeton University.

Shawn Nussbaum. Shawn is a technical leader and consummate problem solver with over 30 years of experience developing software and leading high-performing teams. Shawn worked at Return Path from 2010 to 2019, where he led Product and Engineering and was responsible for setting the vision and culture of the organization, extracting meaning from email data, and applying technology as a force-multiplier to solve interesting and difficult problems for customers. Prior to Return Path, he helped launch two Internet companies and was an advisor and technical director for a consortium of insurance companies. Shawn cofounded Bolster in 2020, a company focused on helping startups and scaleups grow, develop, and scale their leadership teams and boards. Shawn contributed to *Startup CXO: A Field Guide to Scaling Up Your Company's Critical Functions and Teams* (Wiley, 2021), sharing his experience, tips, and best practices for CTO/CPOs for creating effective product development leaders and culture as they scale up the technology/product function. He believes that empathy and usefulness are the keys to remarkable products.